Jared Weiss

The Slow Death of the Instant

Sproketbox Entertainment

www.jaredweiss.blogspot.com
www.sprocketbox.yolasite.com

Published by:
Sprocketbox Entertainment 2010
Chicago Illinois

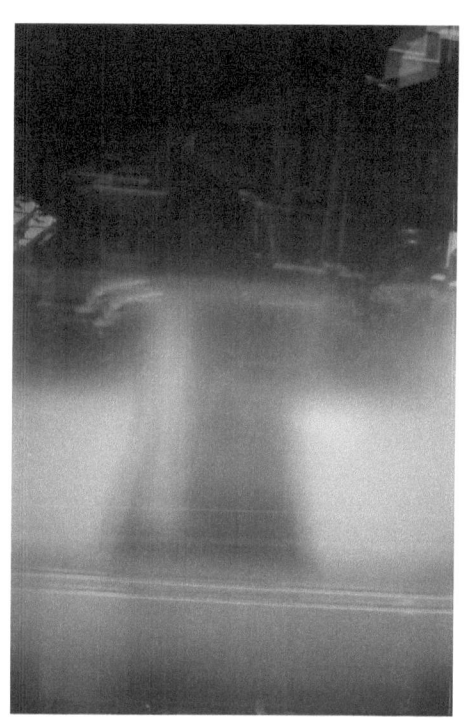

Artist Statement

Ghosts surround us. They exist in ink, in words, in memories. Ultimately, for me, they exist in paint and the photographic image. The idea of a ghost consists of something that has once existed in entirety and has since partially disappeared, leaving an echo that rings through time. Paint and photography are ways to temporarily freeze that echo and redirect it into future consciousness.

With absence, a trace is felt through residual memory being transferred to certain form. Painting is a means of expressing this form, a way of locking an image or an idea into a semi-static state, thus allowing it to perpetuate. When a paintbrush leaves a mark, that mark has the potential to stay set in place for thousands of years. It stands as a reference to the paintbrush's absence. Most objects present us with this record of a previous event. Marks carry a trace.

We are constantly looking into the past. When we look at anything we are looking back in time (light travels at a finite speed). This creates an absence that is also a presence. My work references this absent-presence by resembling a hole or void. Alluding to negative space, the Buddhist Non-Ego, the unconscious, or simply the unknown, these holes symbolically present the abstract concept of emptiness. Human conception of this emptiness can only be alluded to symbolically with juxtapositions to a *somethingness* as a duality of opposites.

Upon closer study figures begin to emerge. These figures are hidden by means of low contrast or shape/color alliterations and are painted from antique photographs (literally ghosts of light). With this they, exist on a different level of consciousness; prolonged consciousness as opposed to the glance. They exert a pull on the viewer, requiring longer conscious participation. Once they are experienced they give reference points to navigate the interrelated meaning of figures to abstraction, known to unknown.

Painting

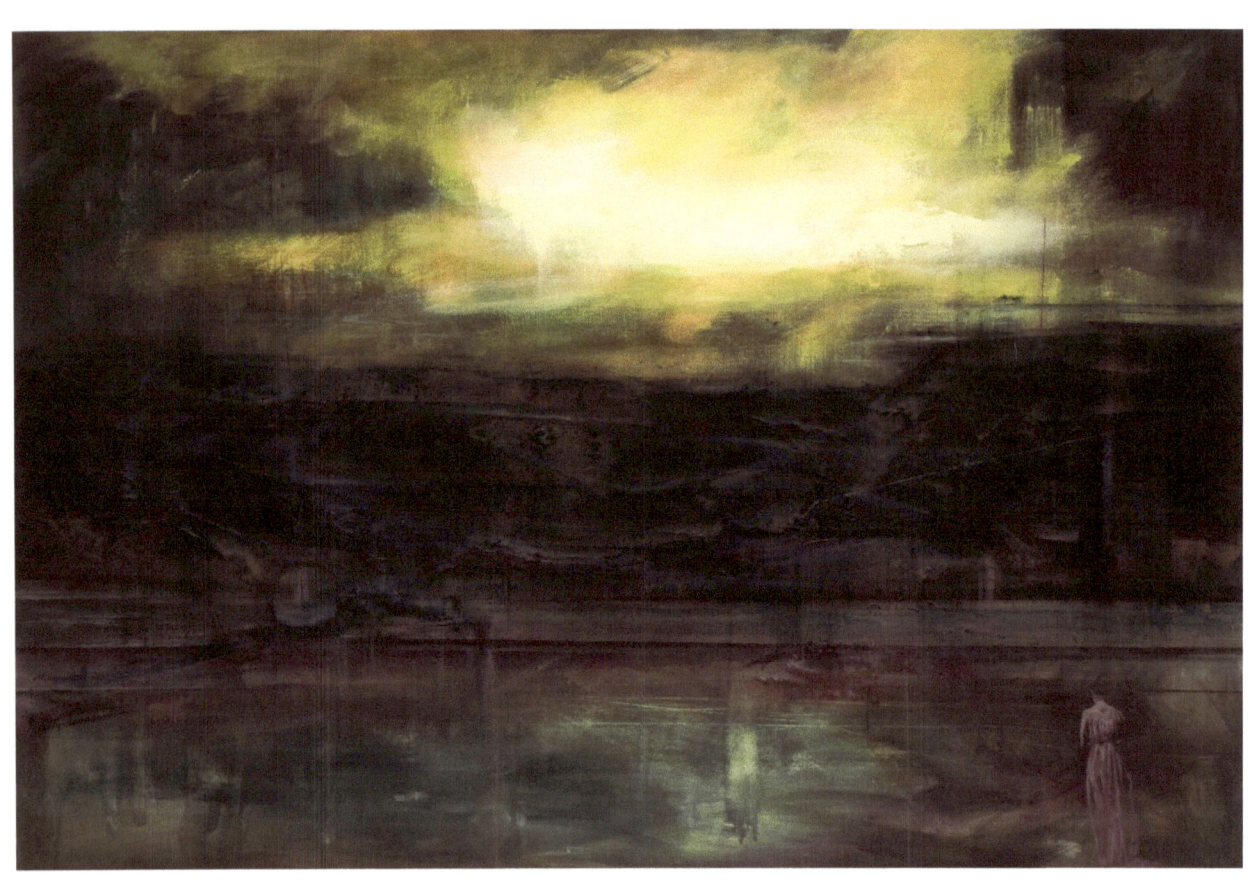

1.

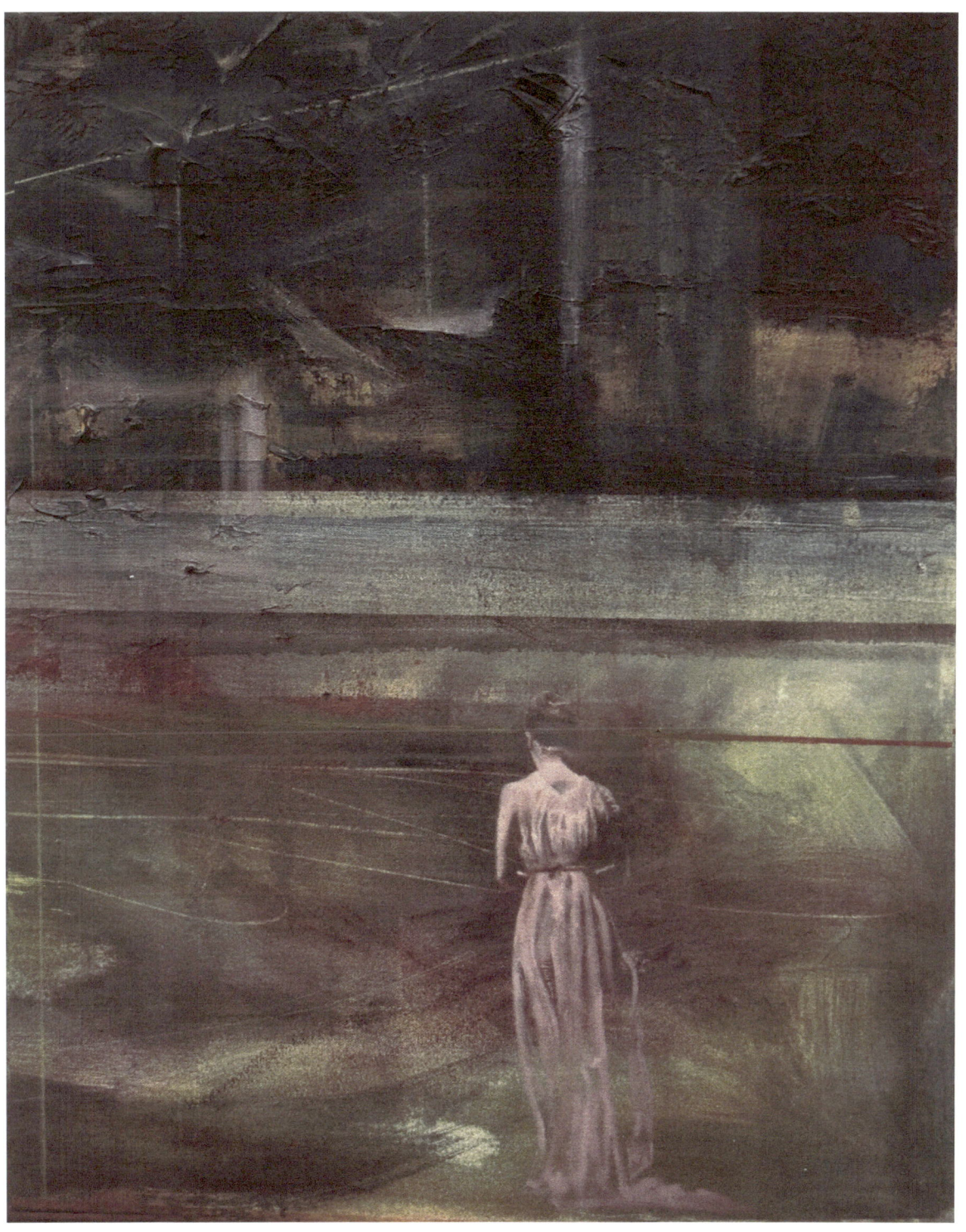

2.

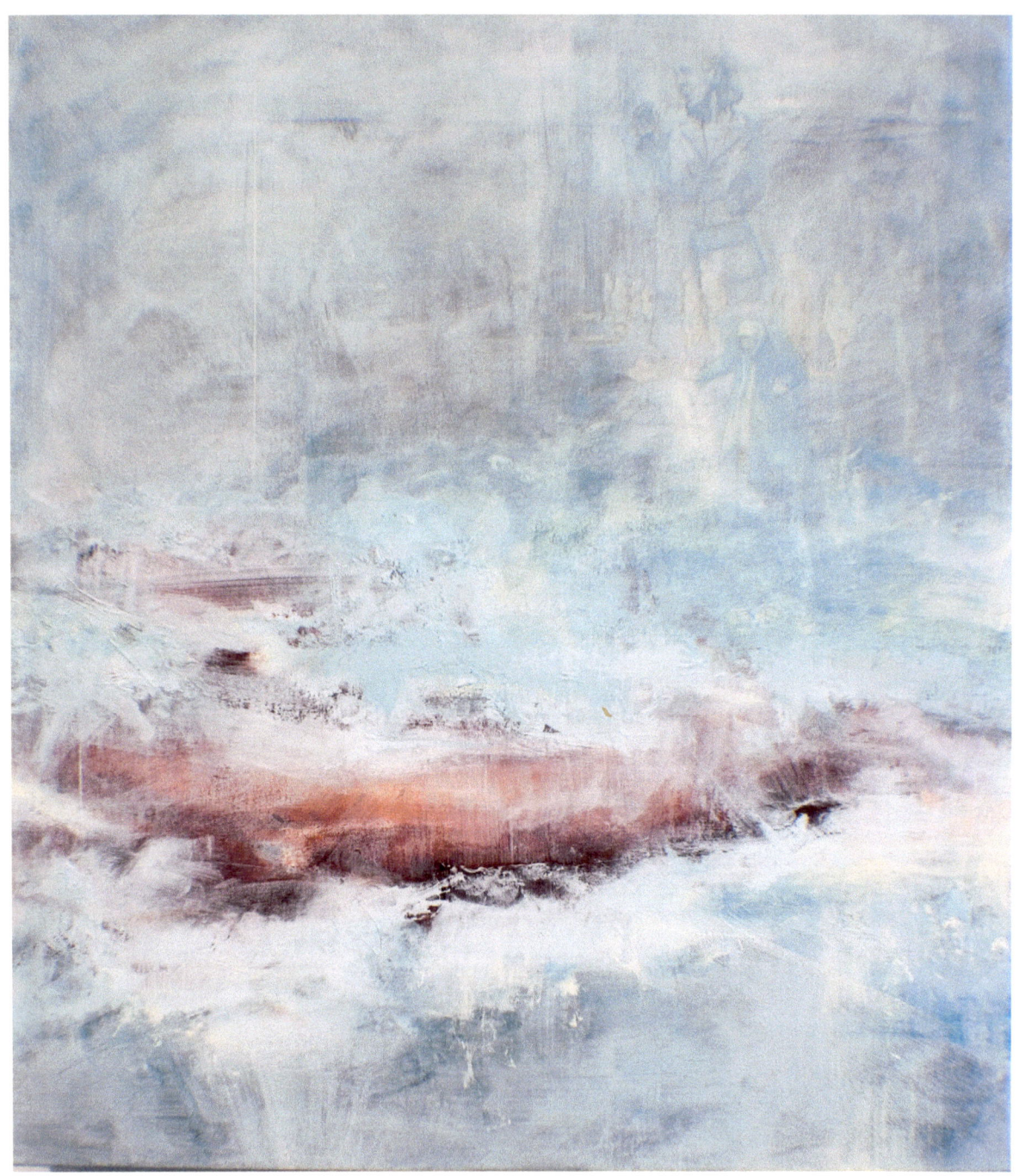

3.

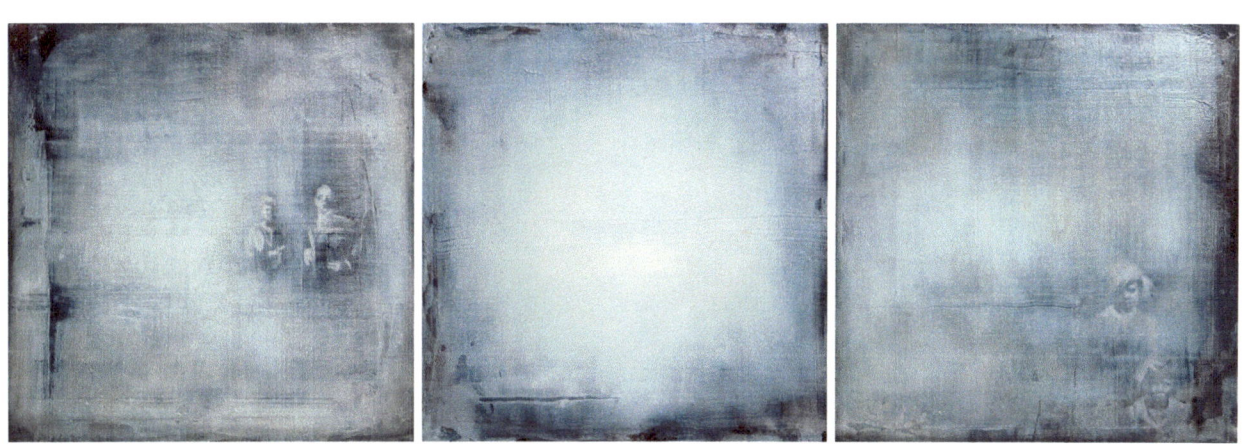

4.

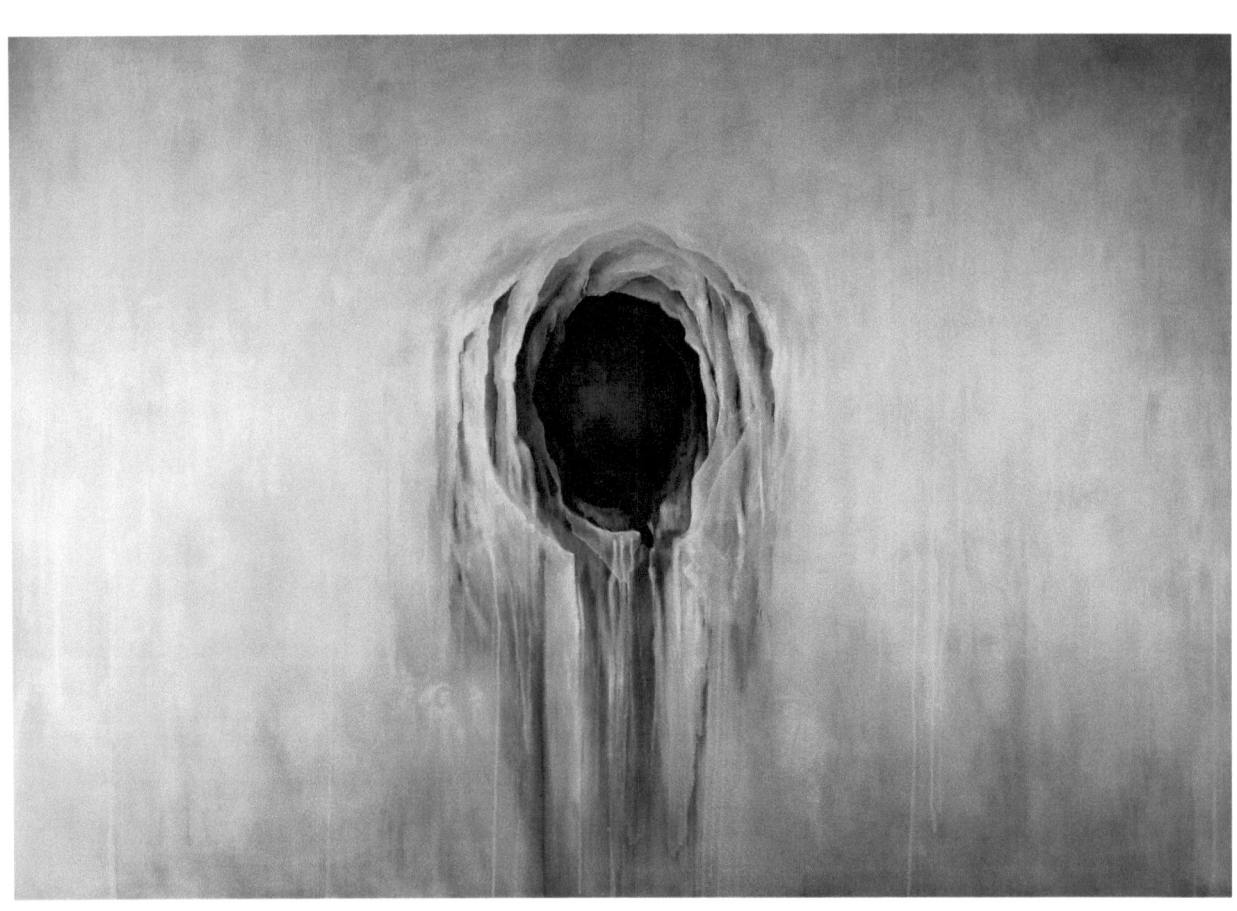

5.

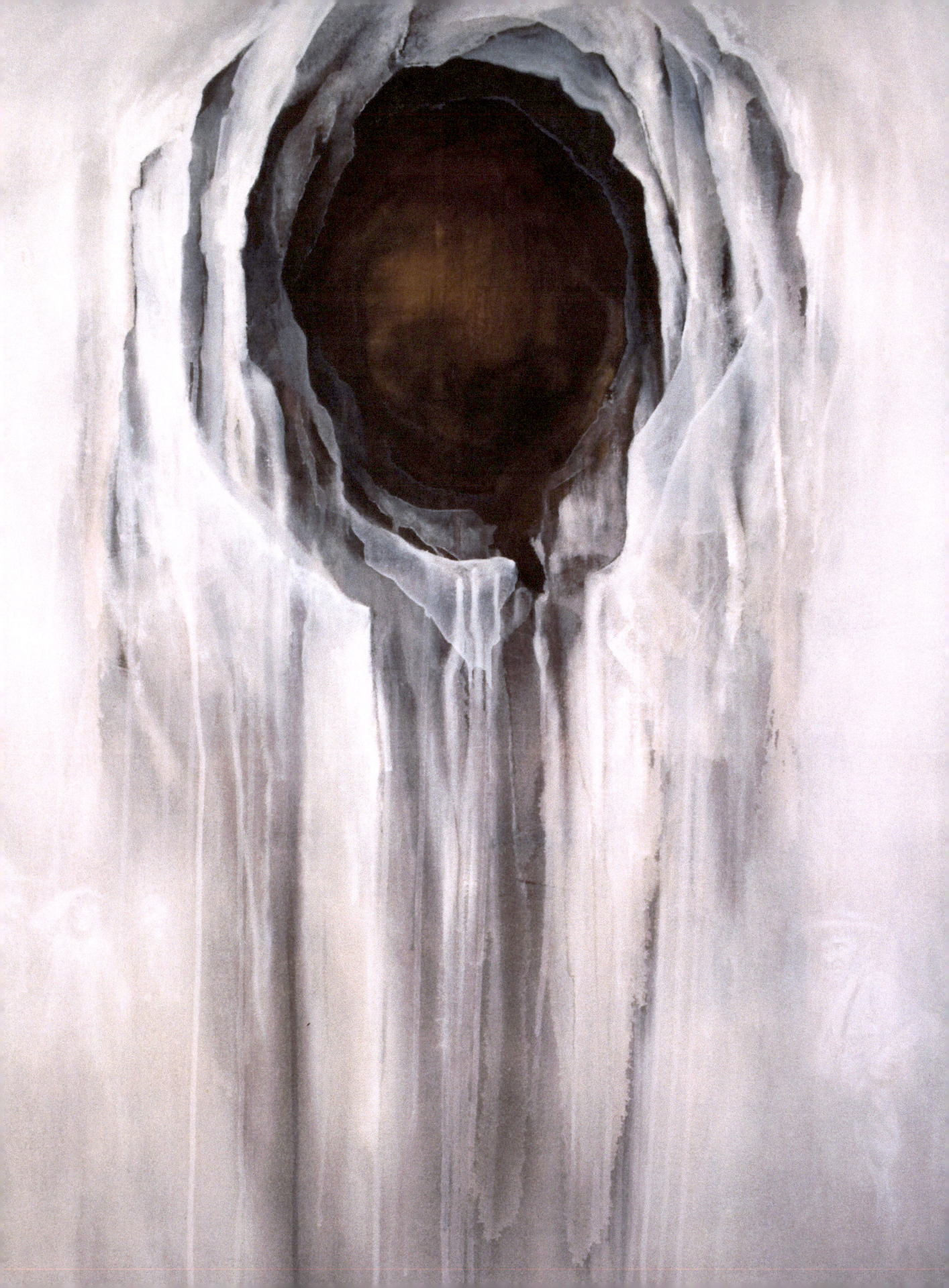

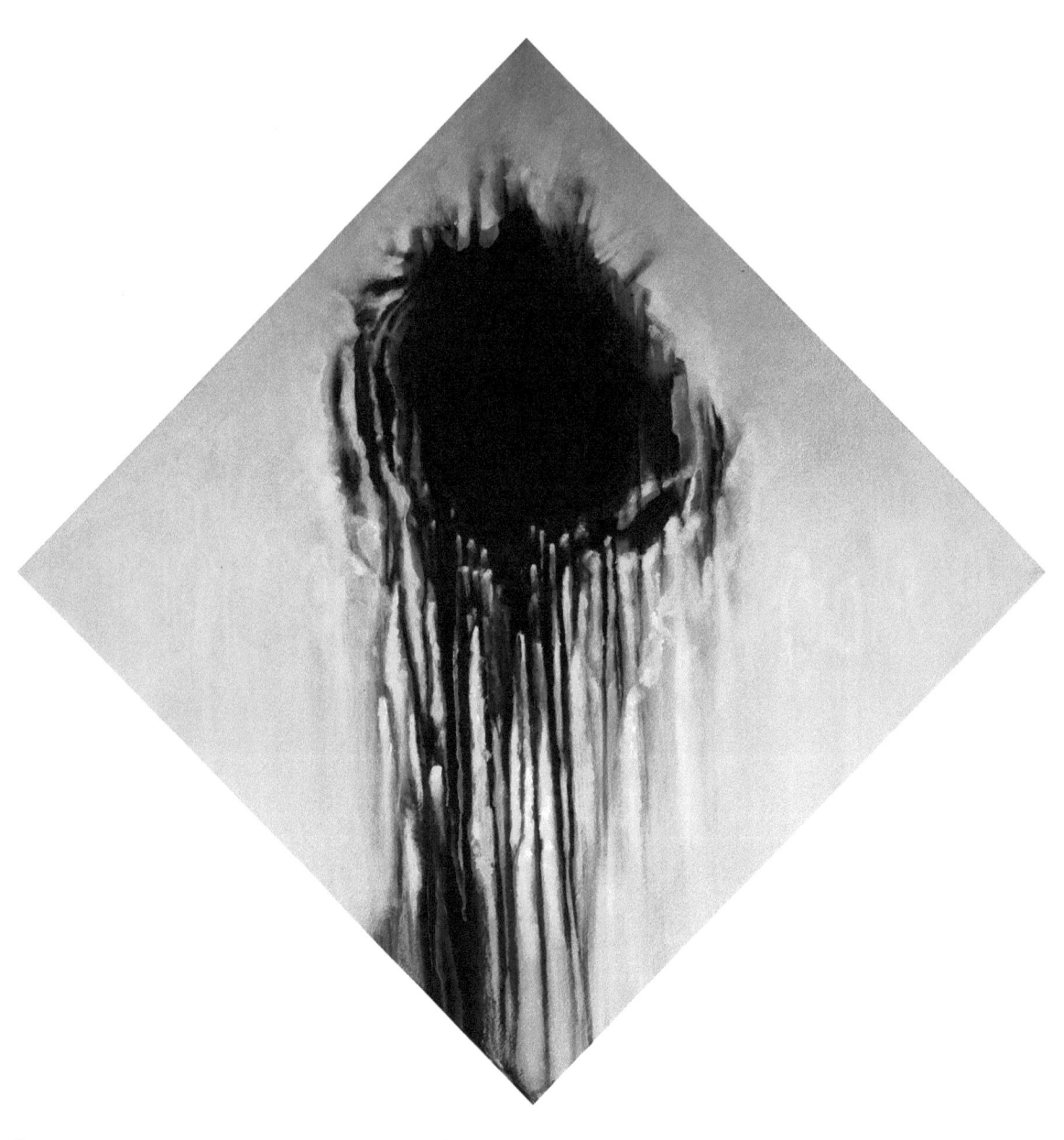

7.

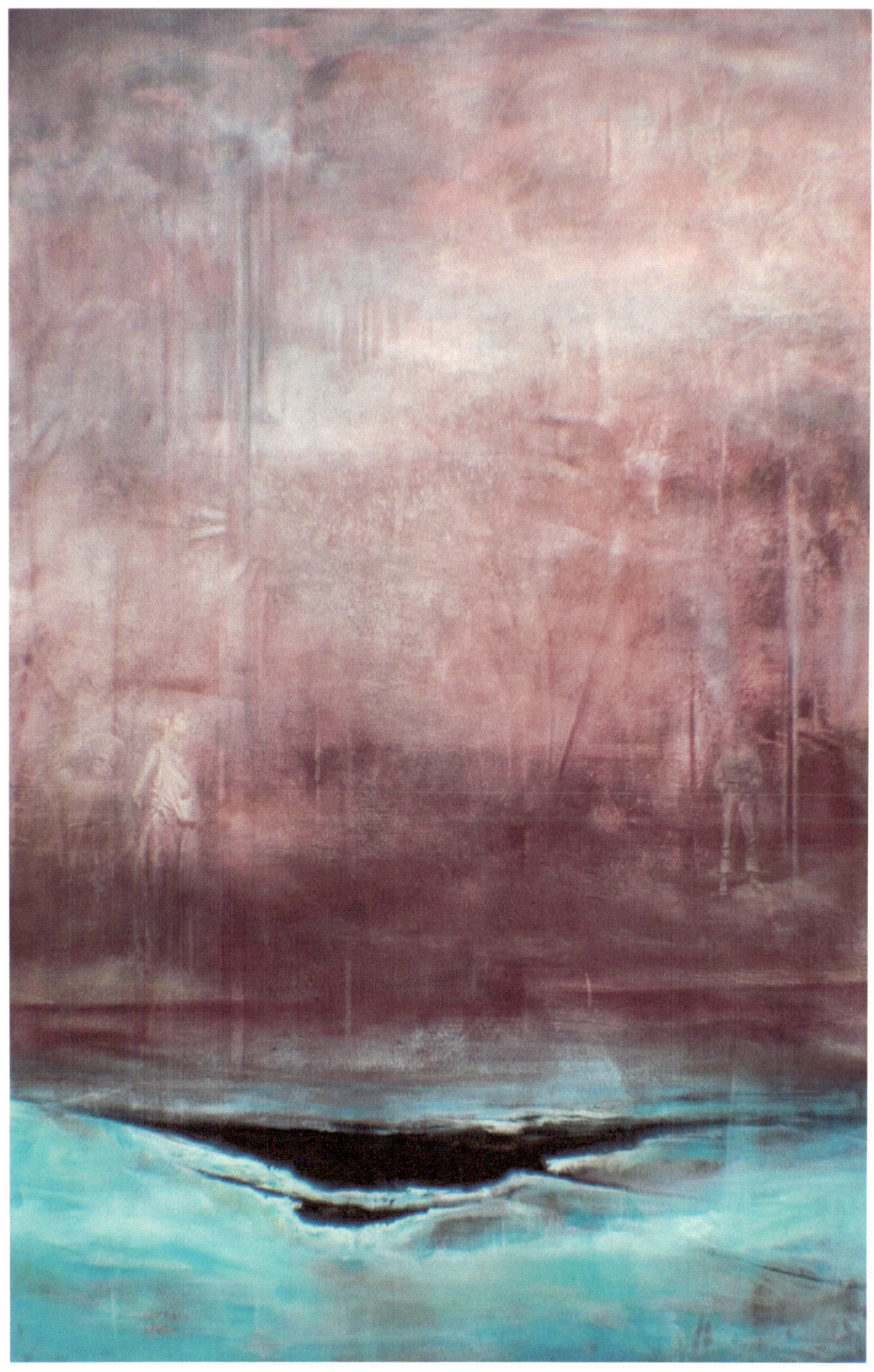

8.

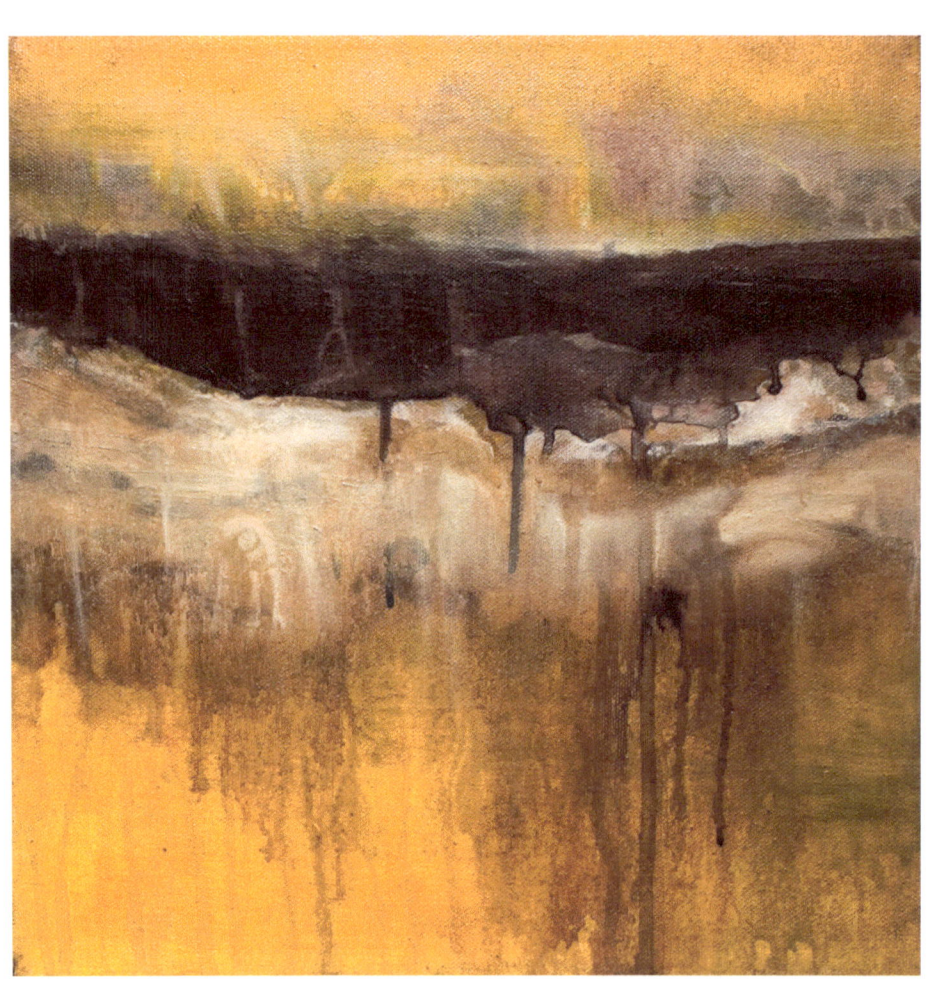

9.

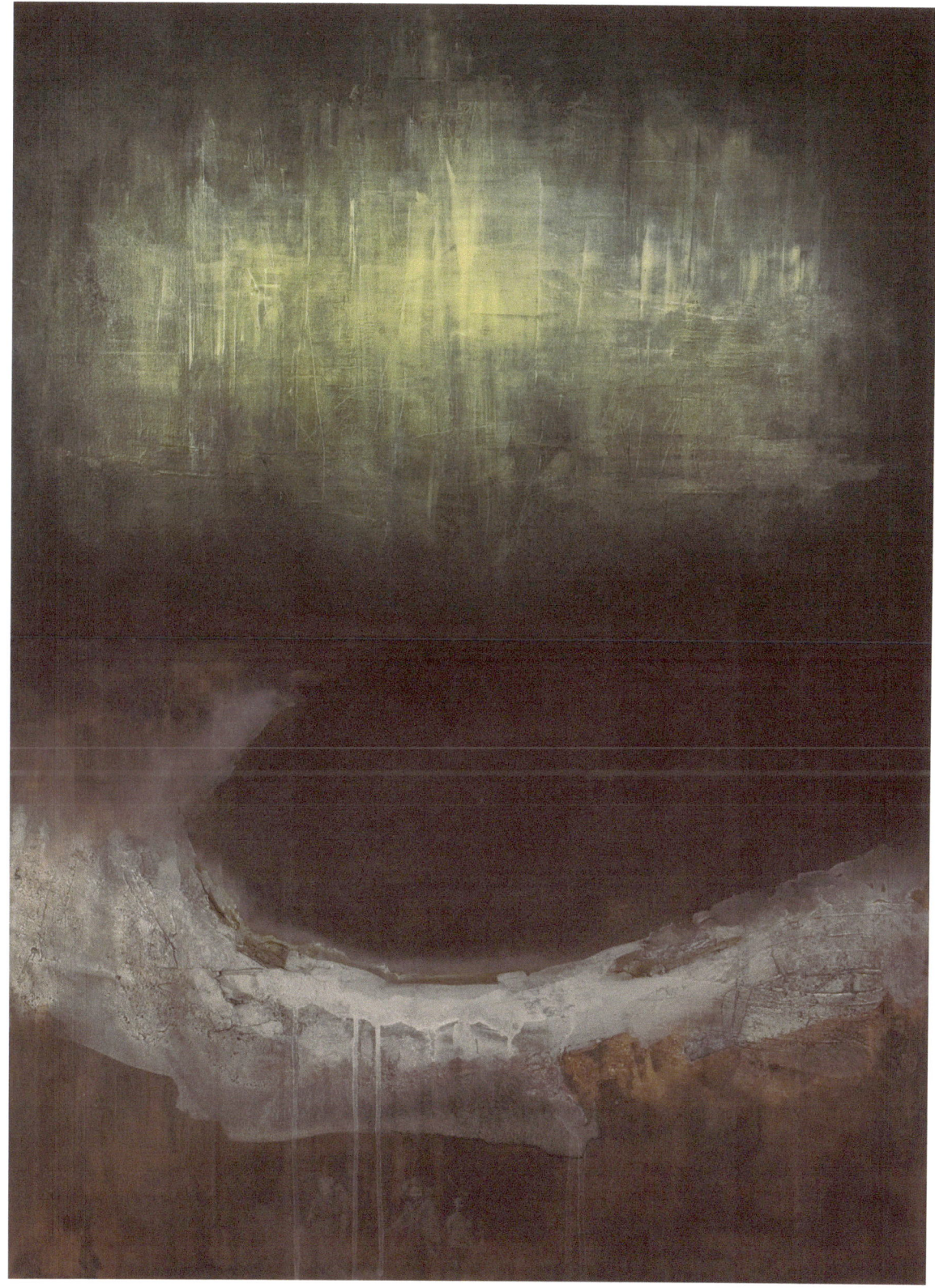

10.

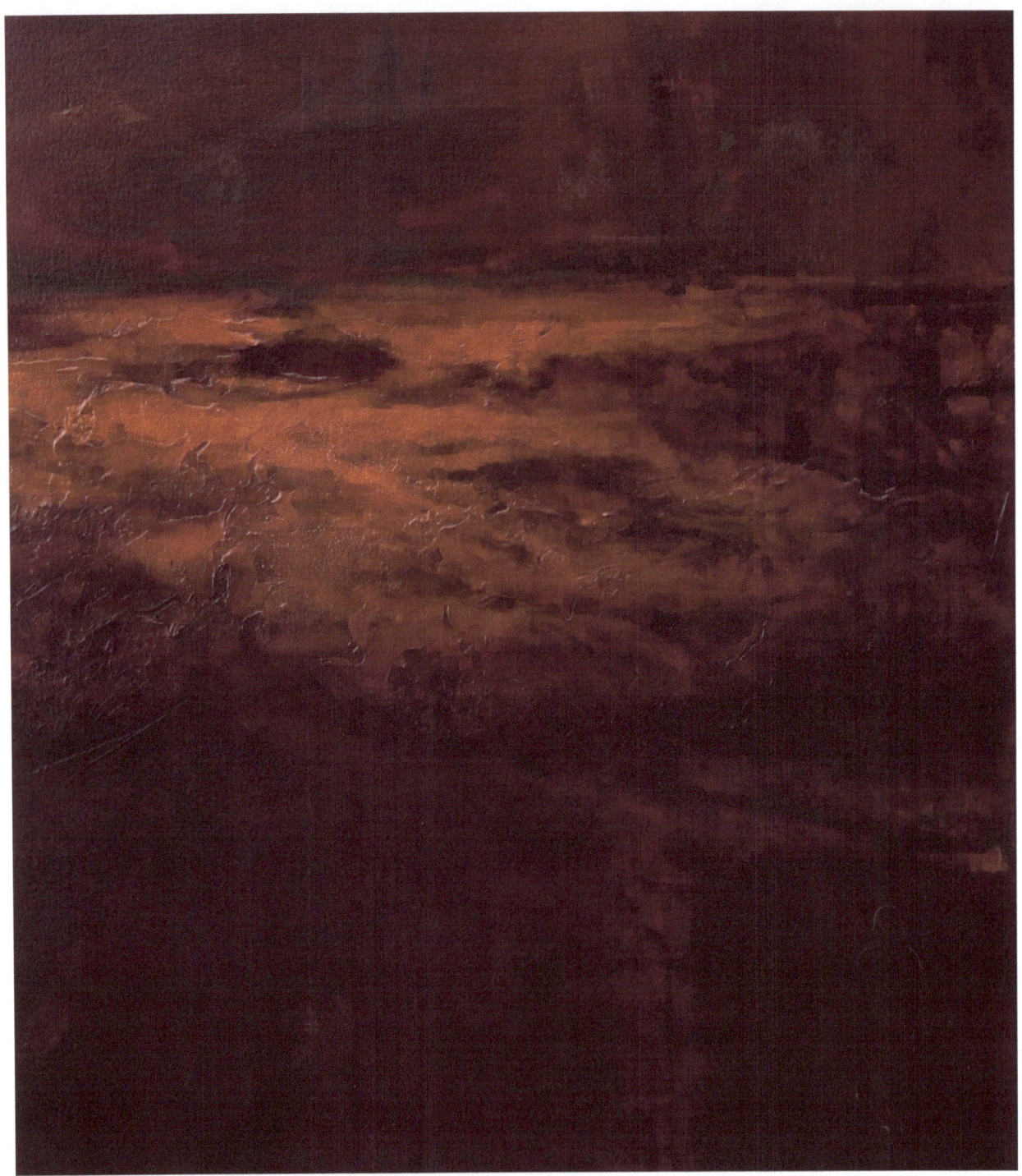

11.

12.

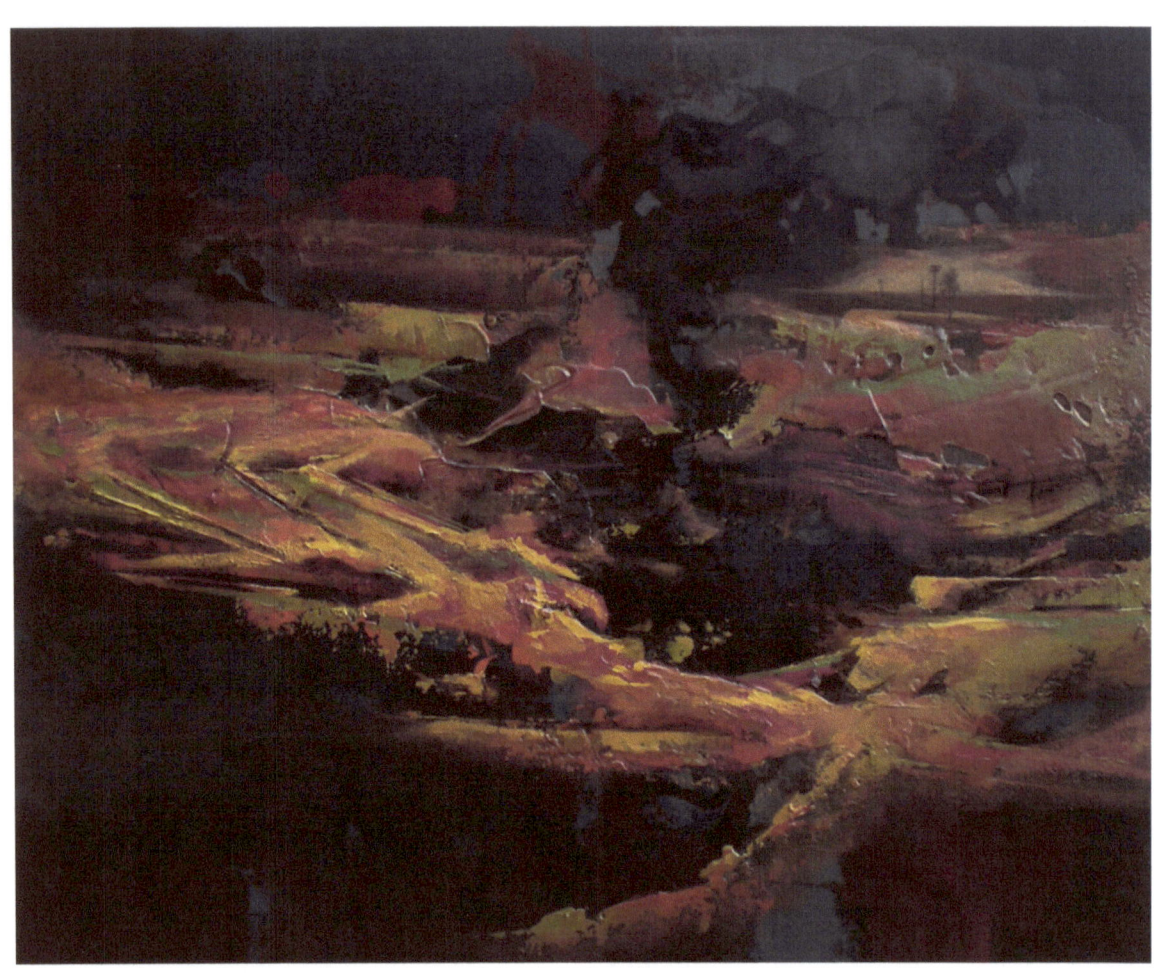

13.

14.

15.

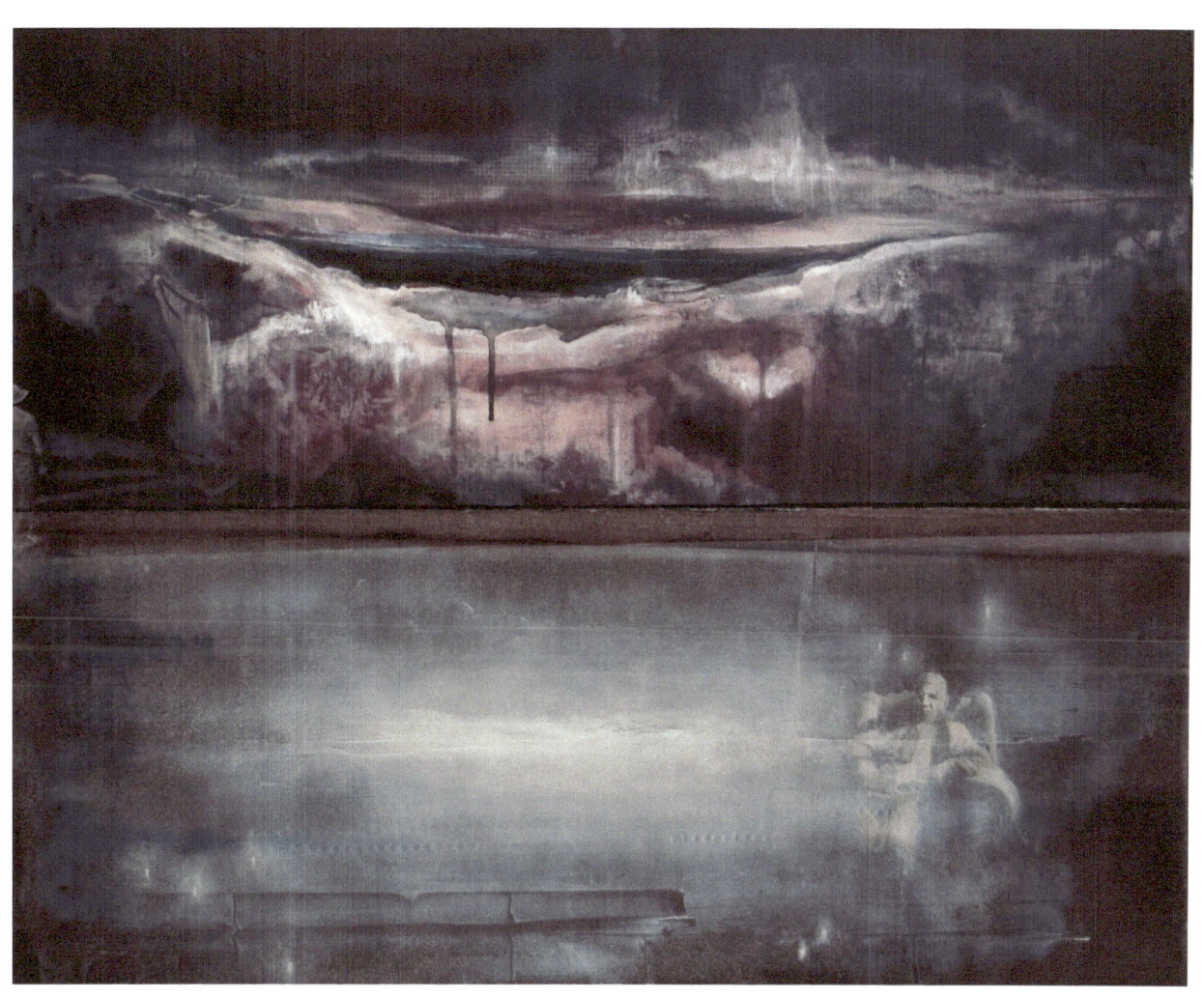

16.

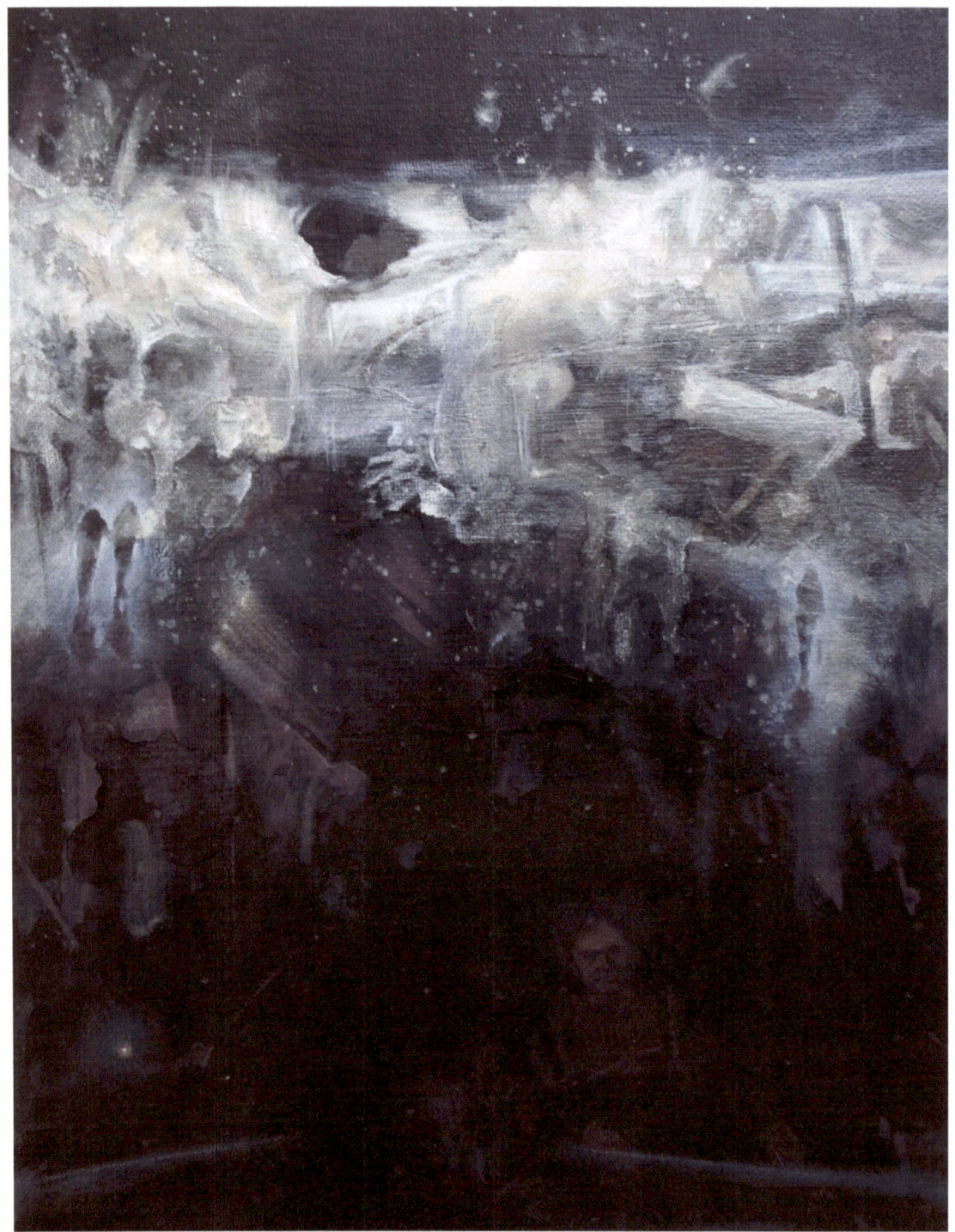

17.

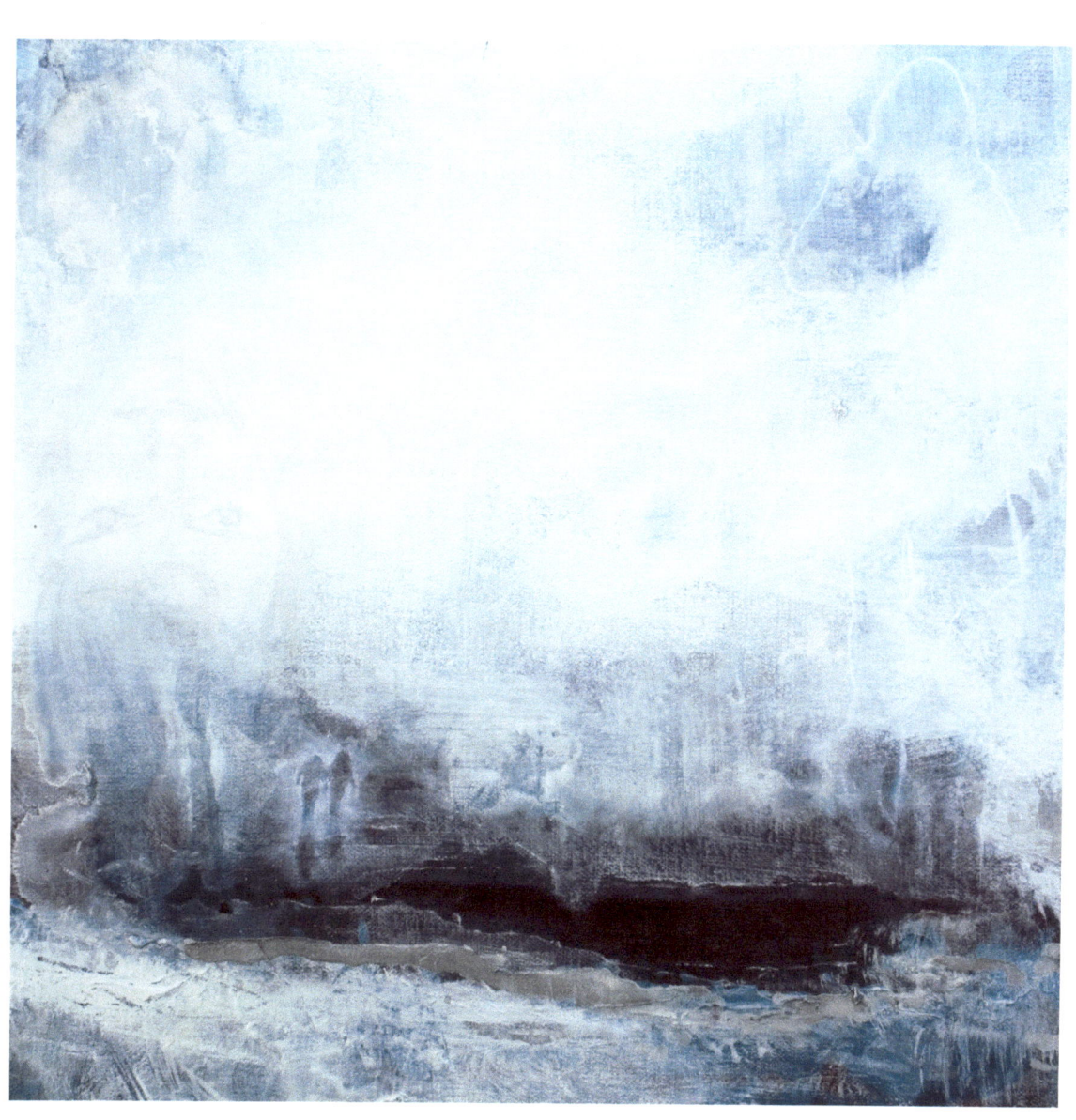

18.

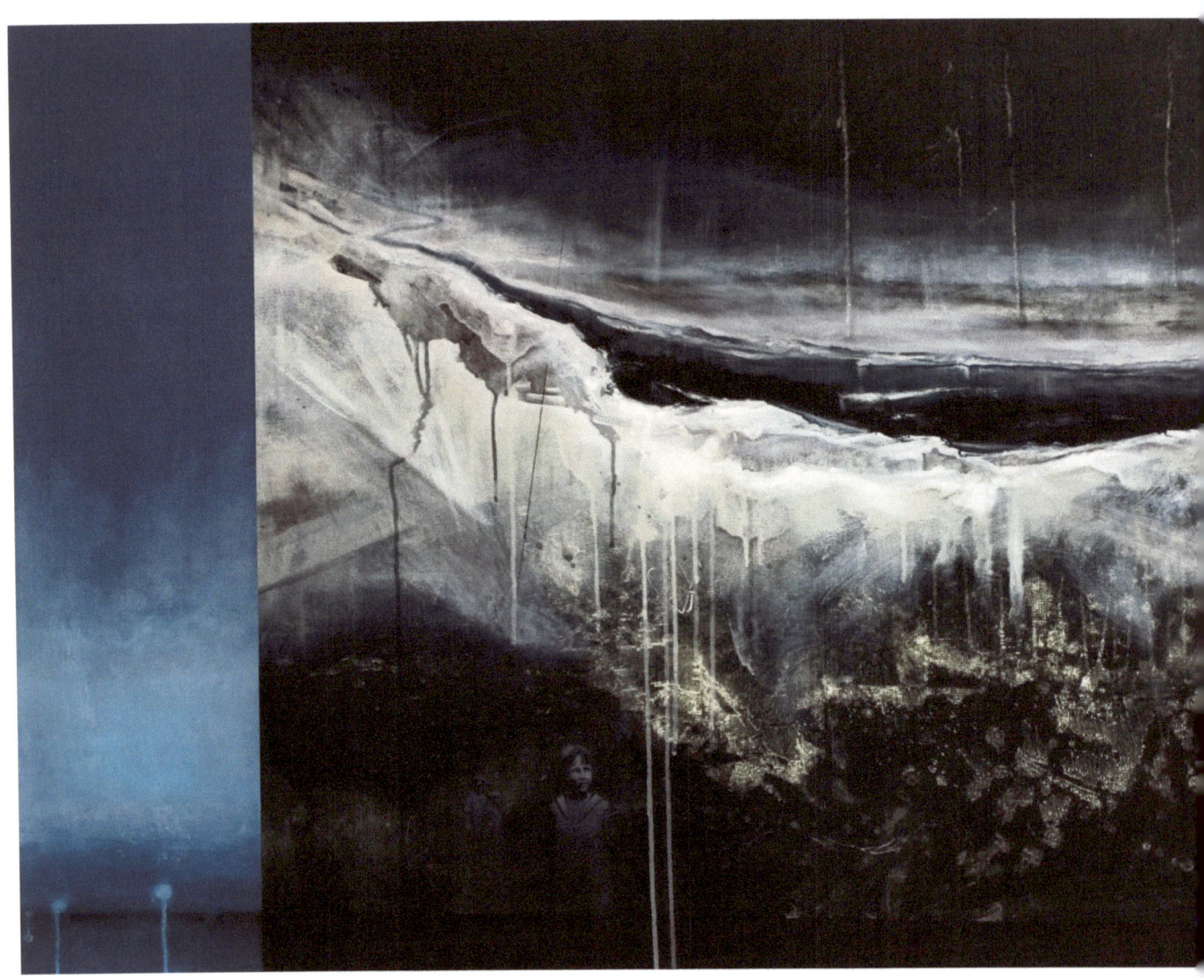

19.

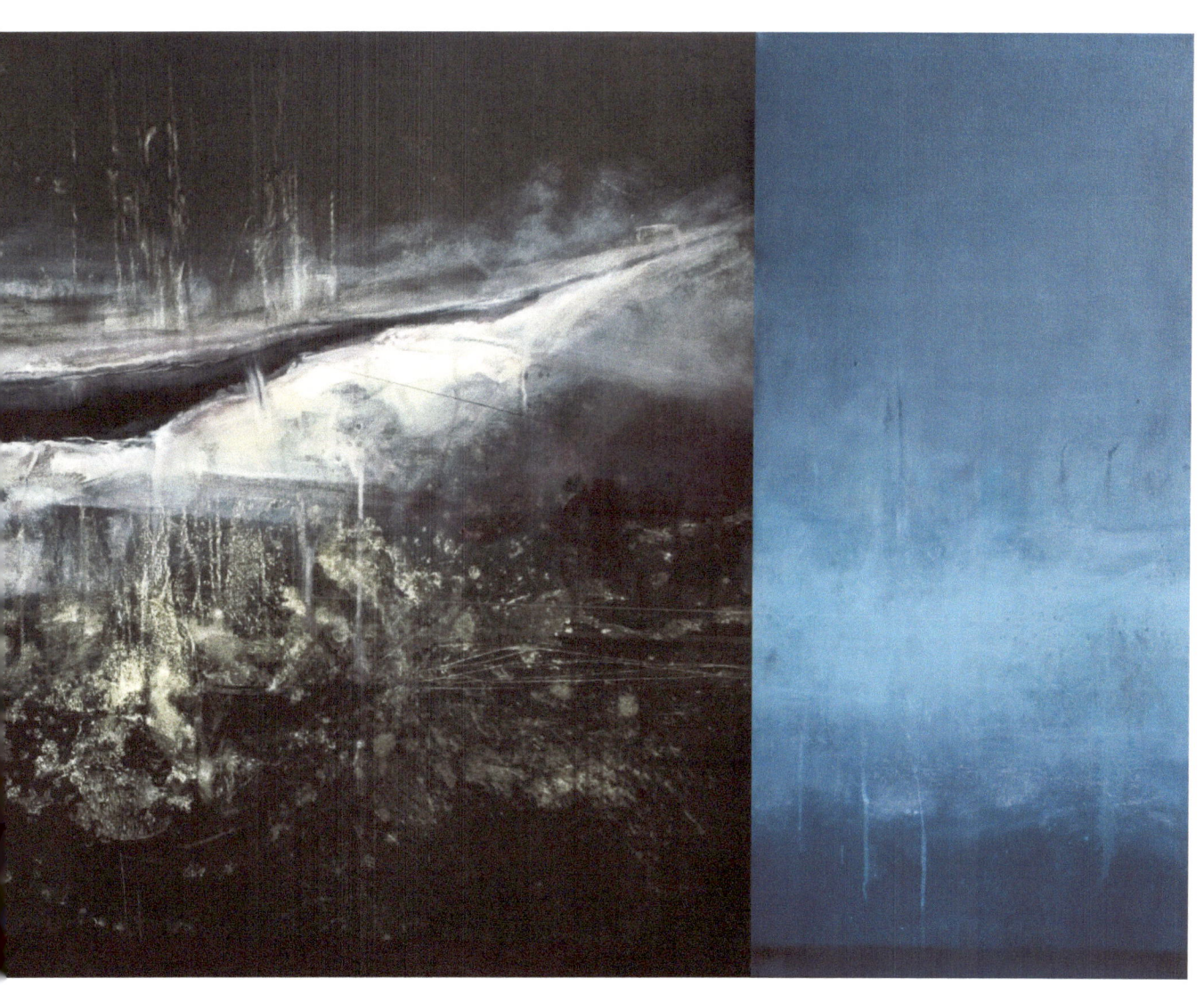

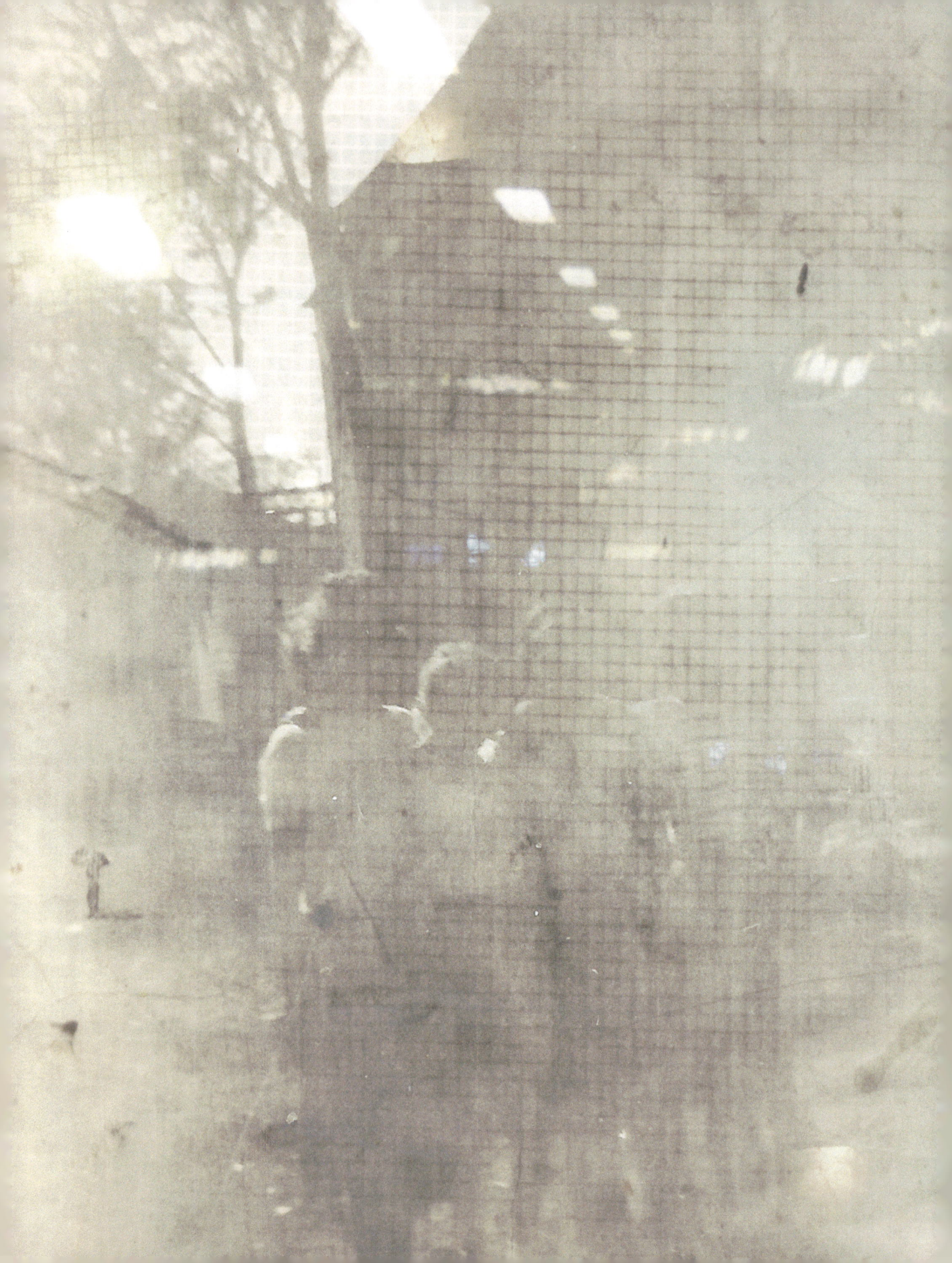

Photo

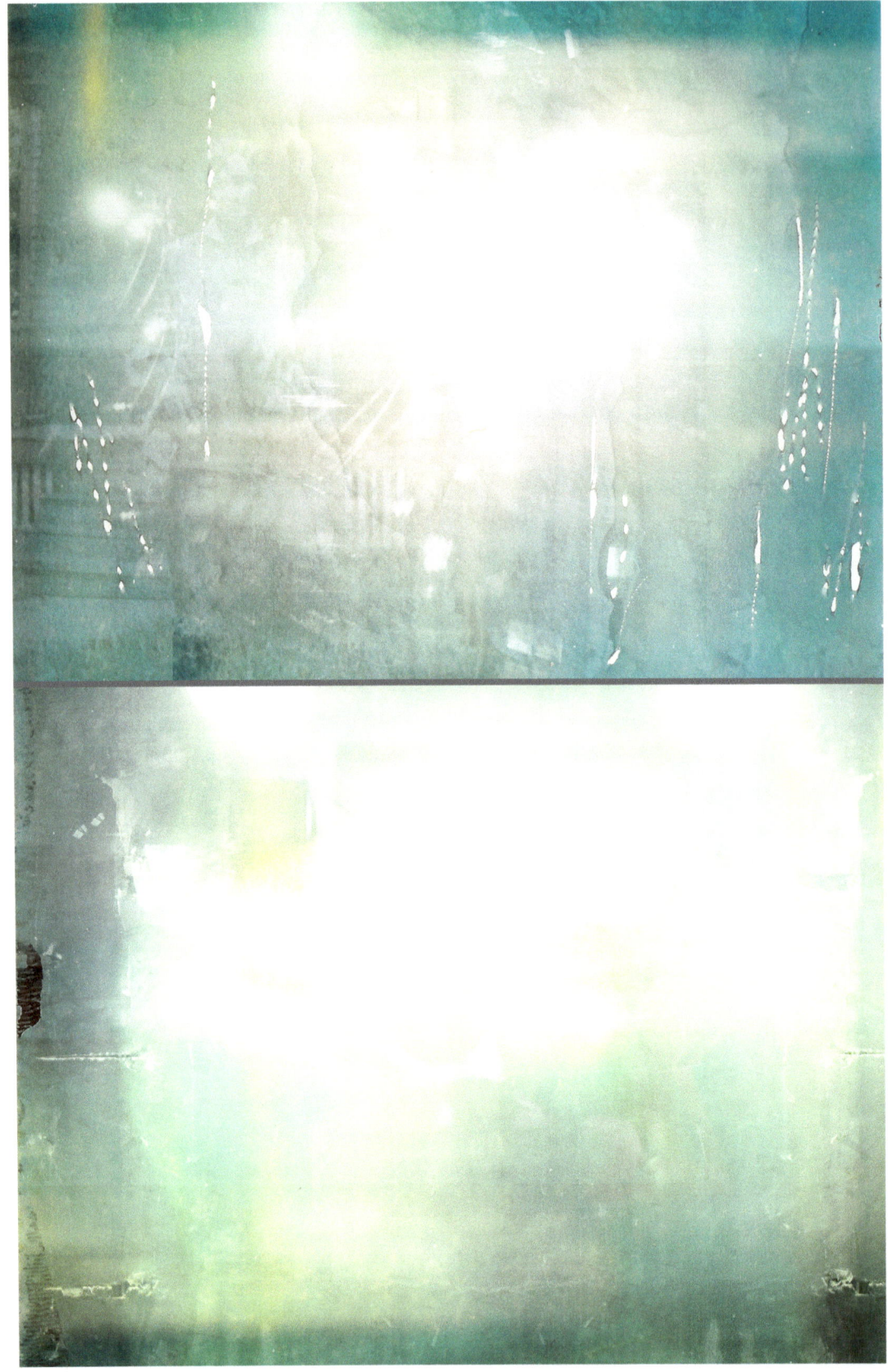

20.

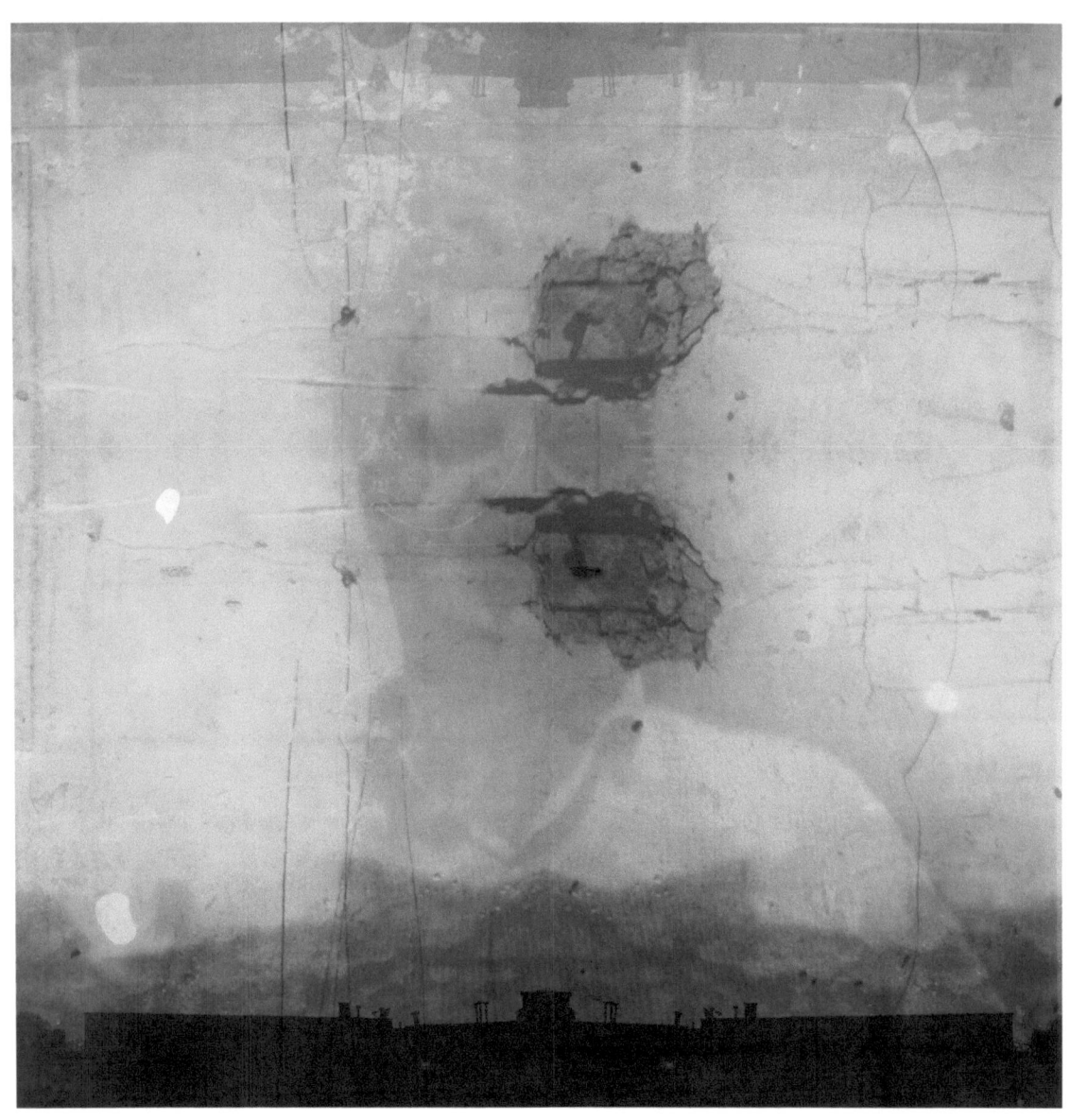

22.

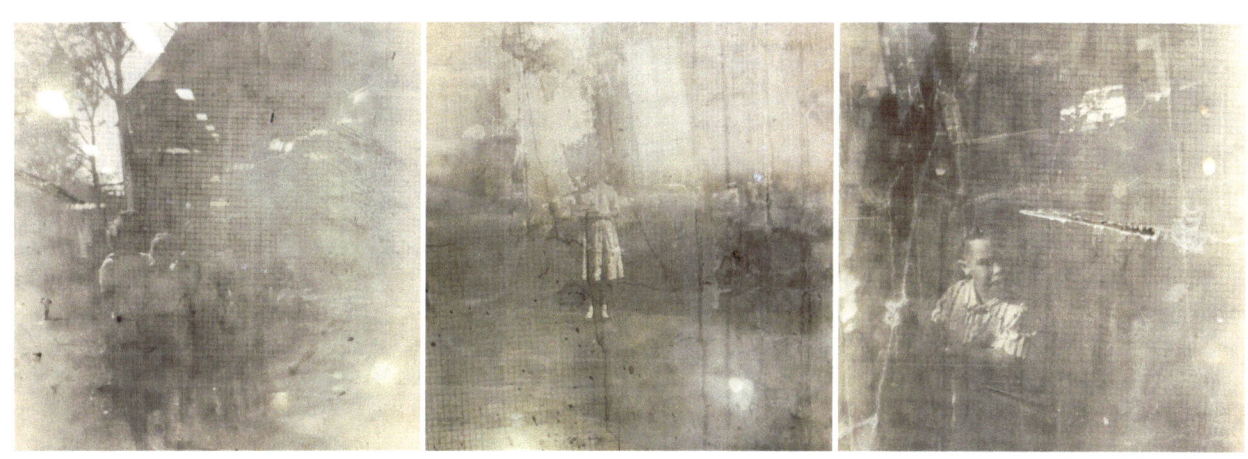

23.

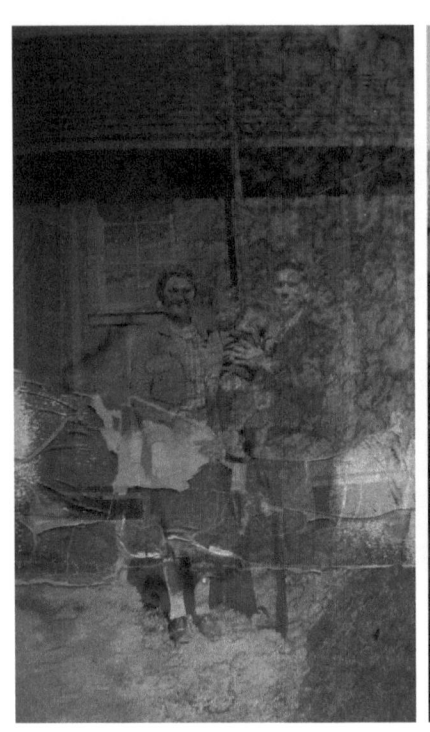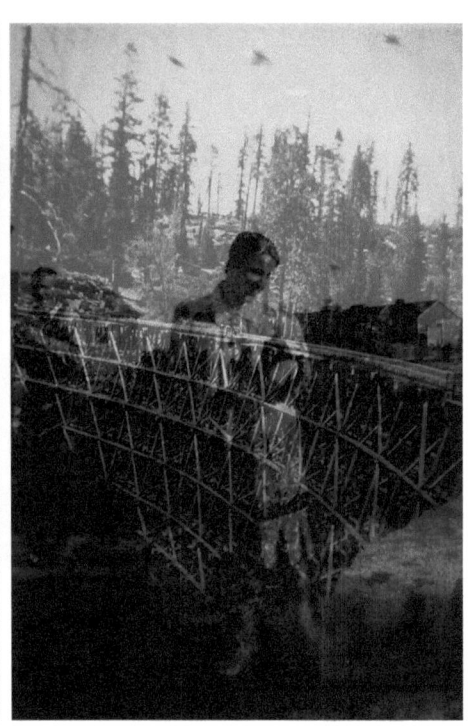

24.

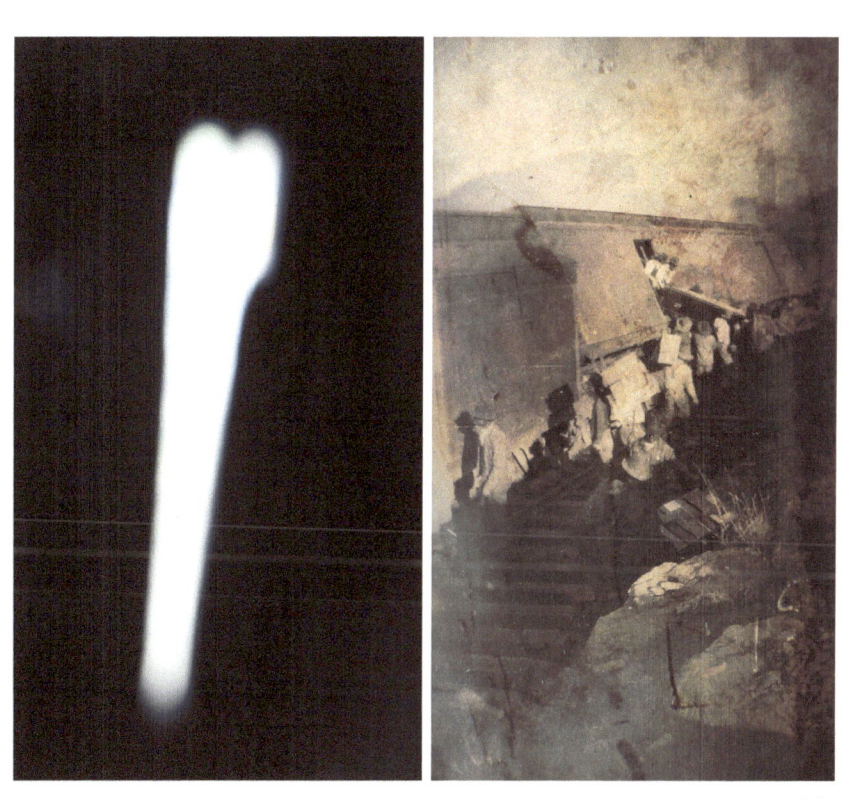

25.

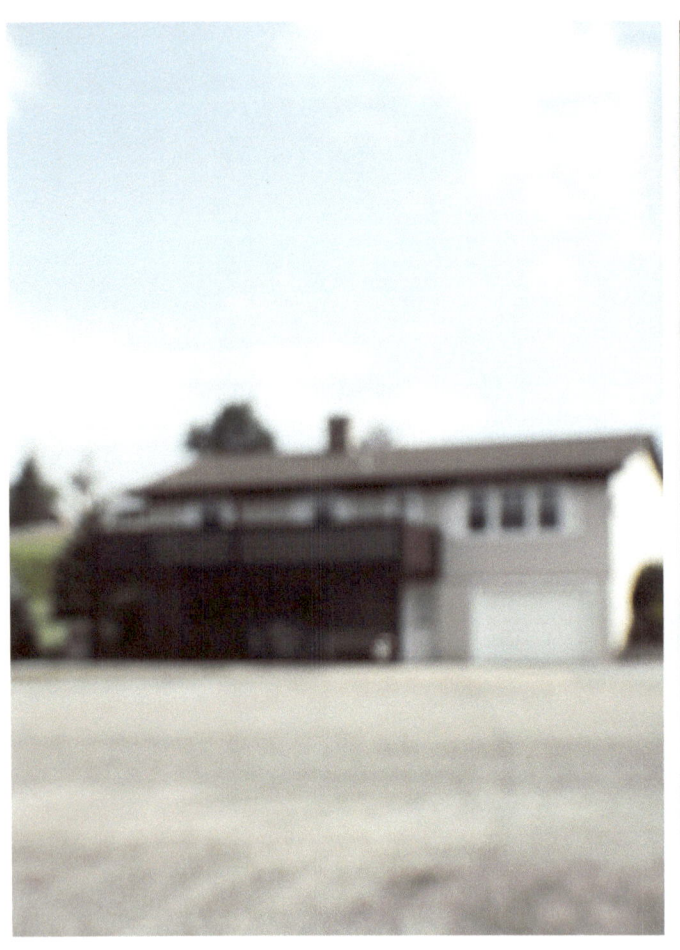
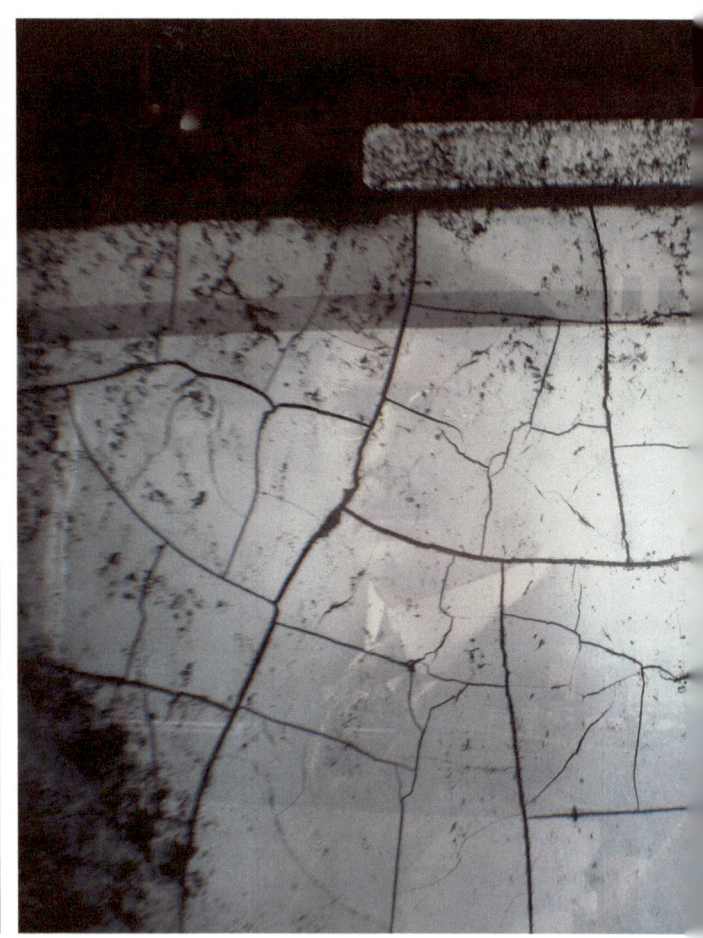

26.

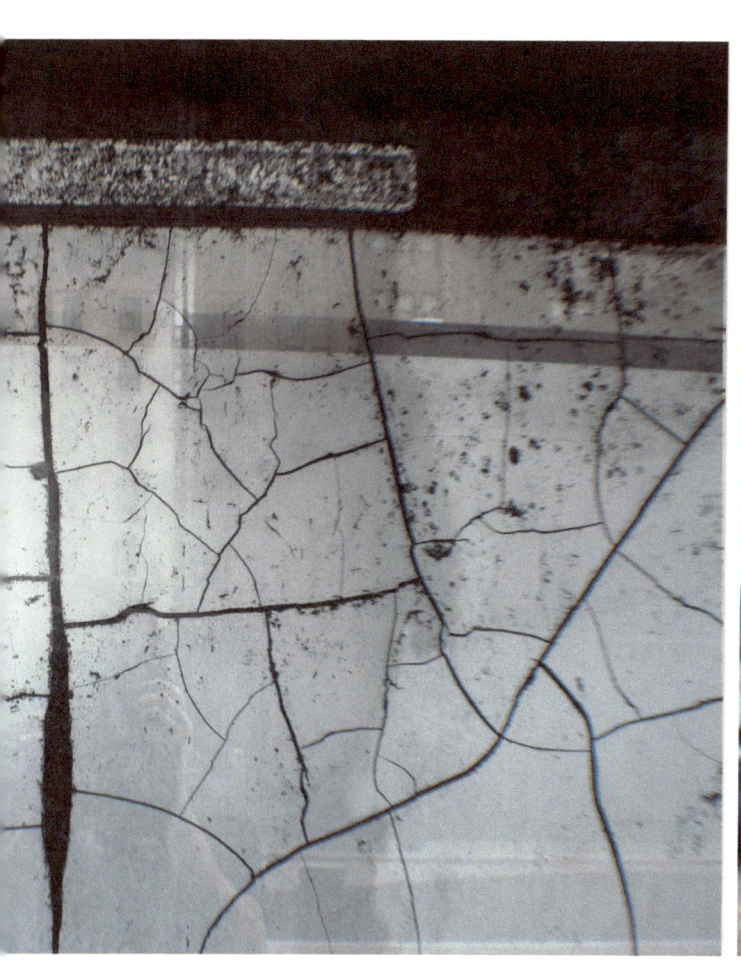
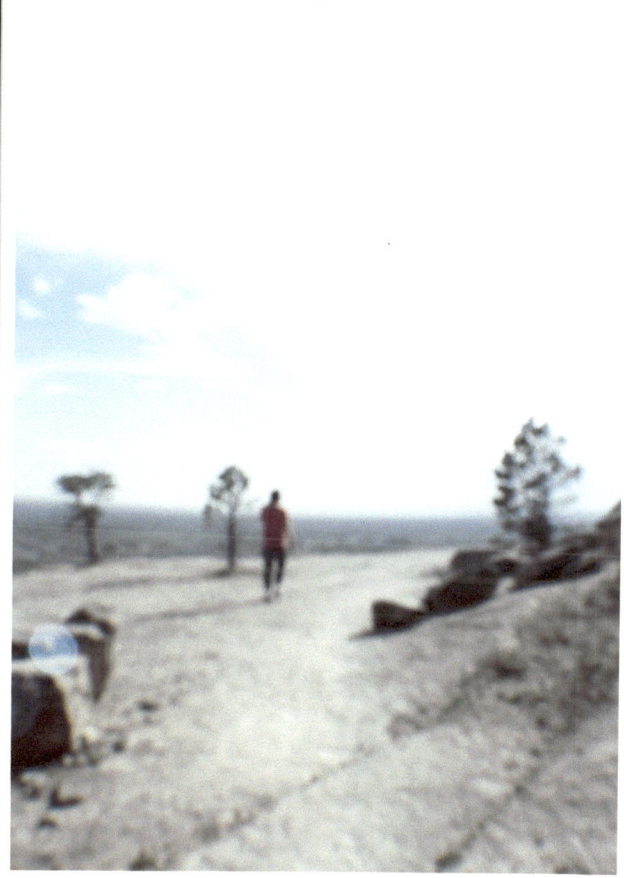

27.

28.

29.

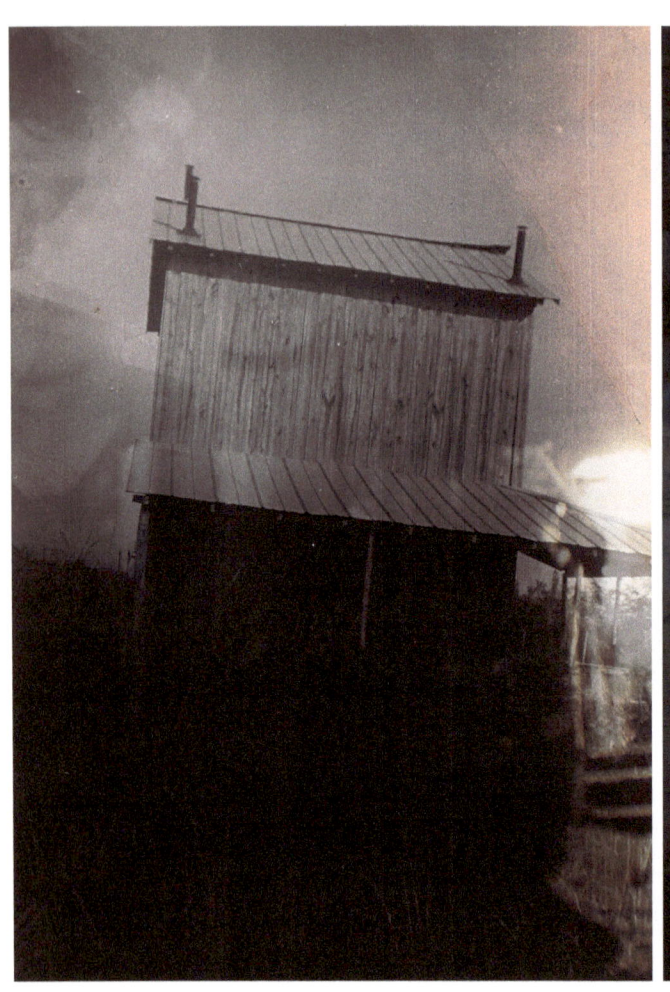 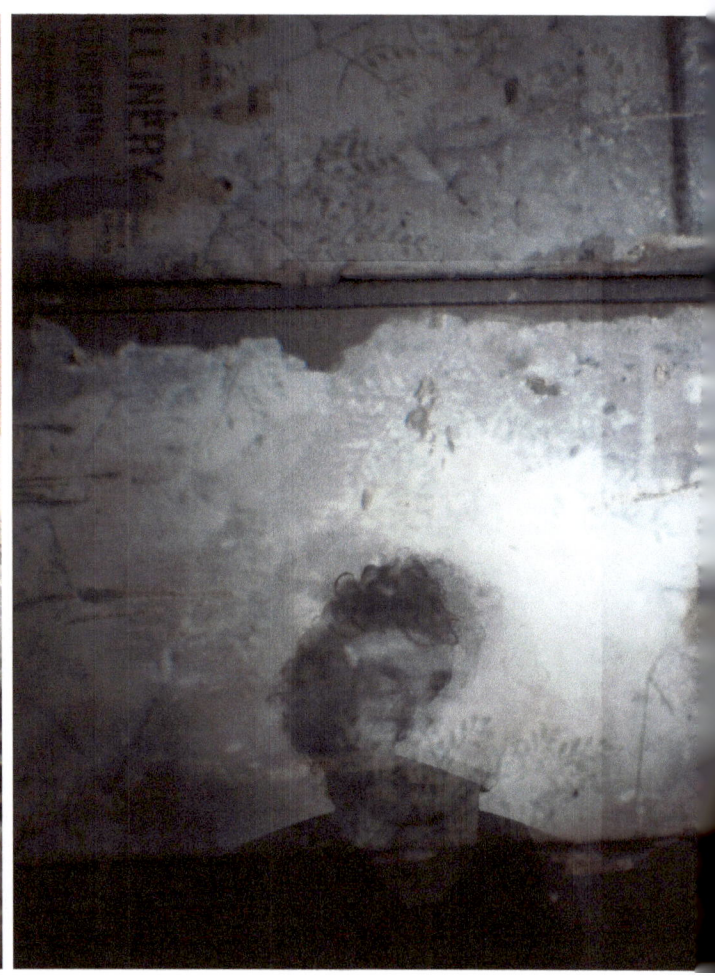

30.

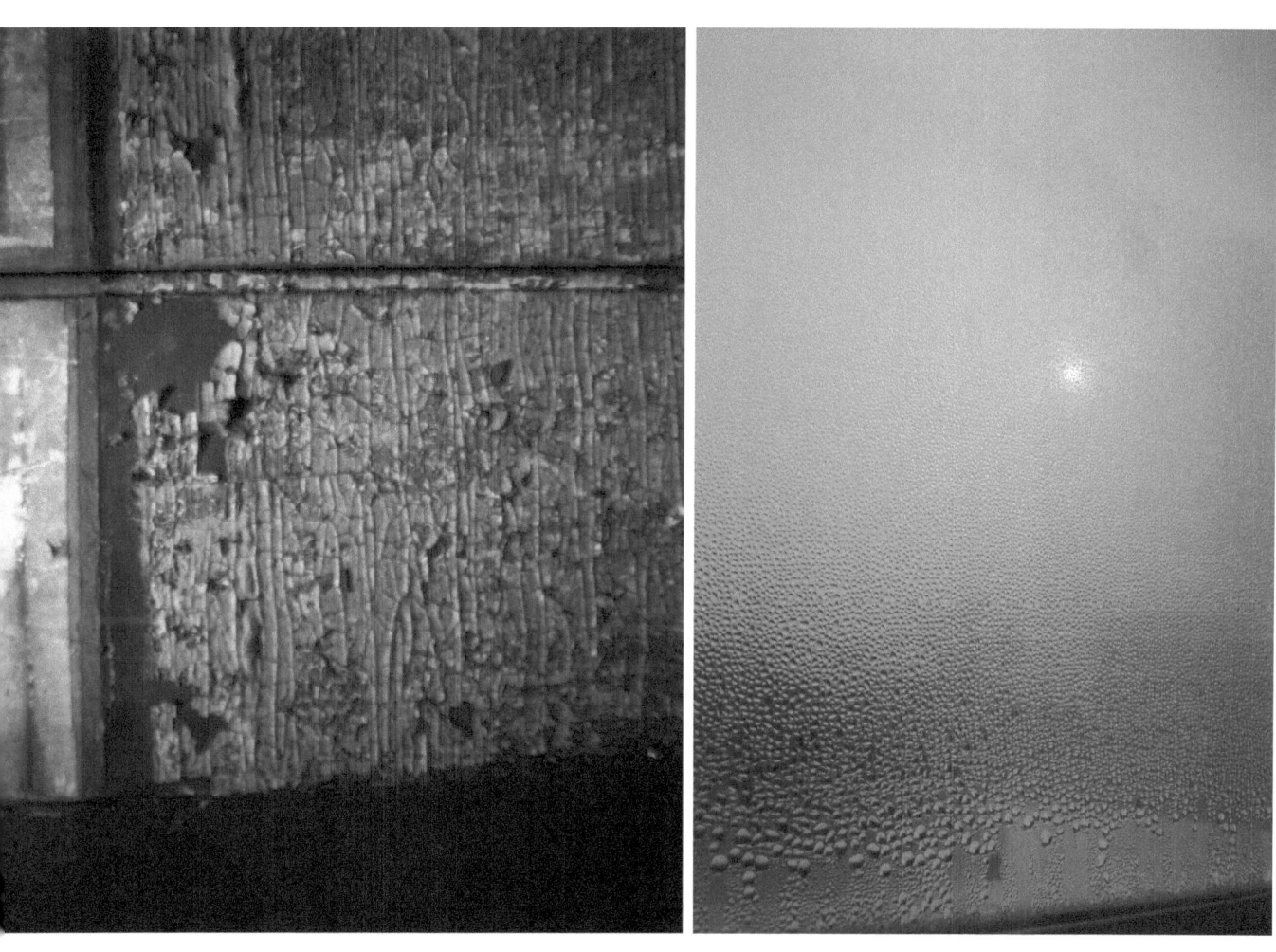

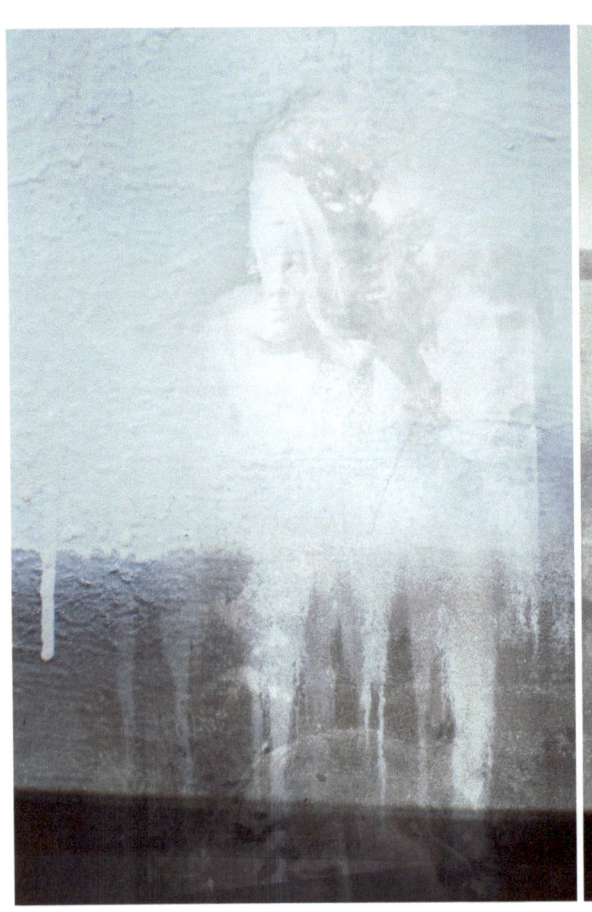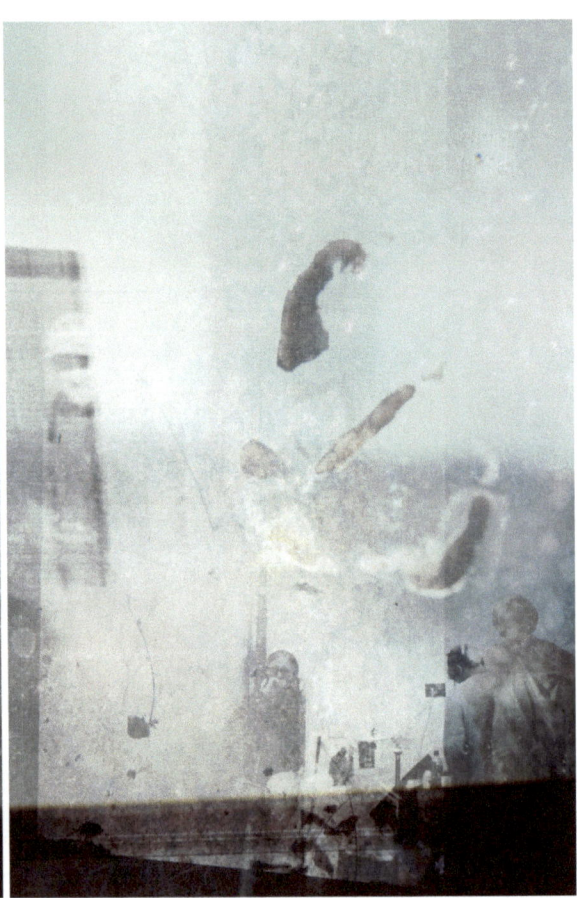

31.

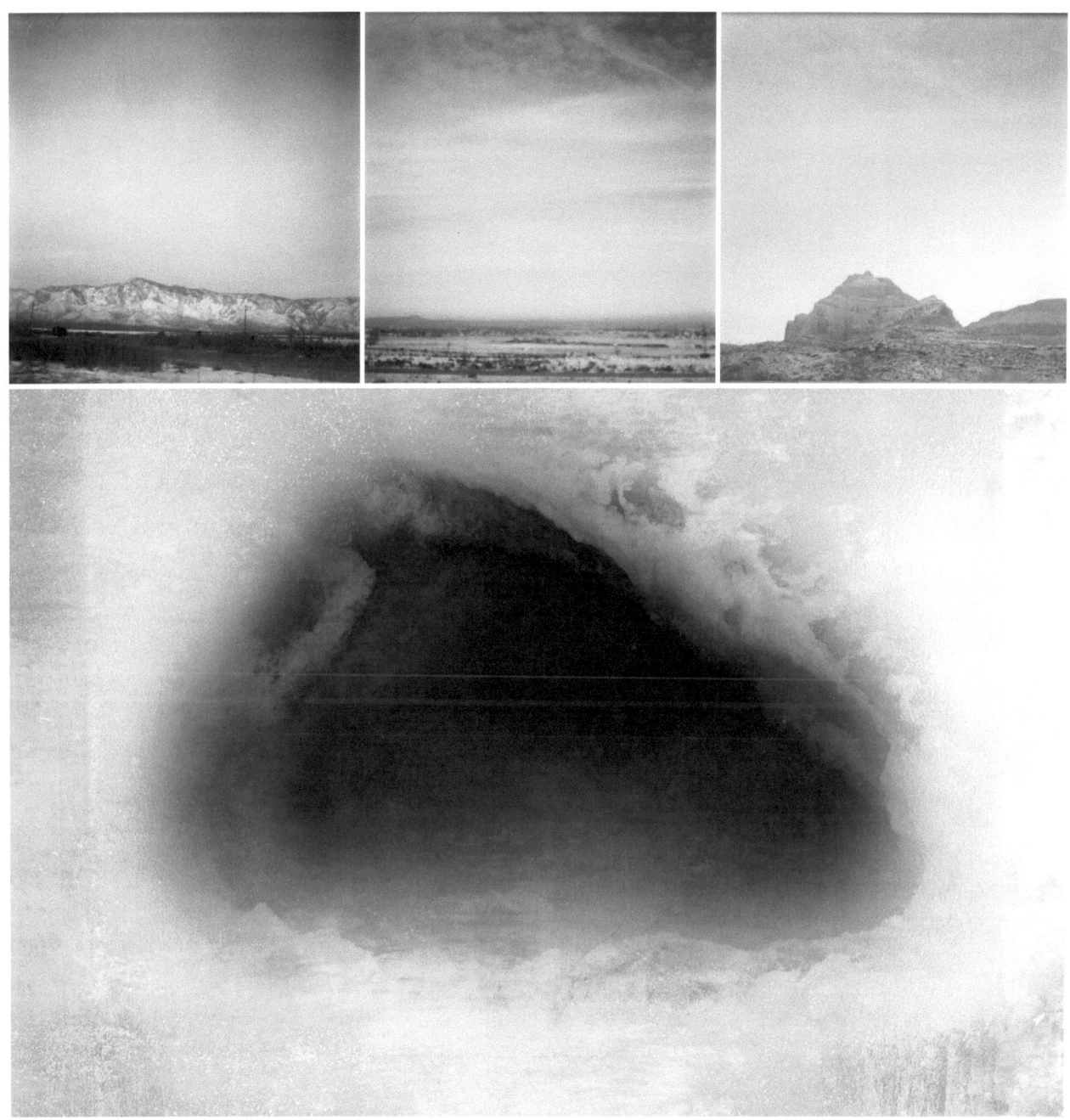

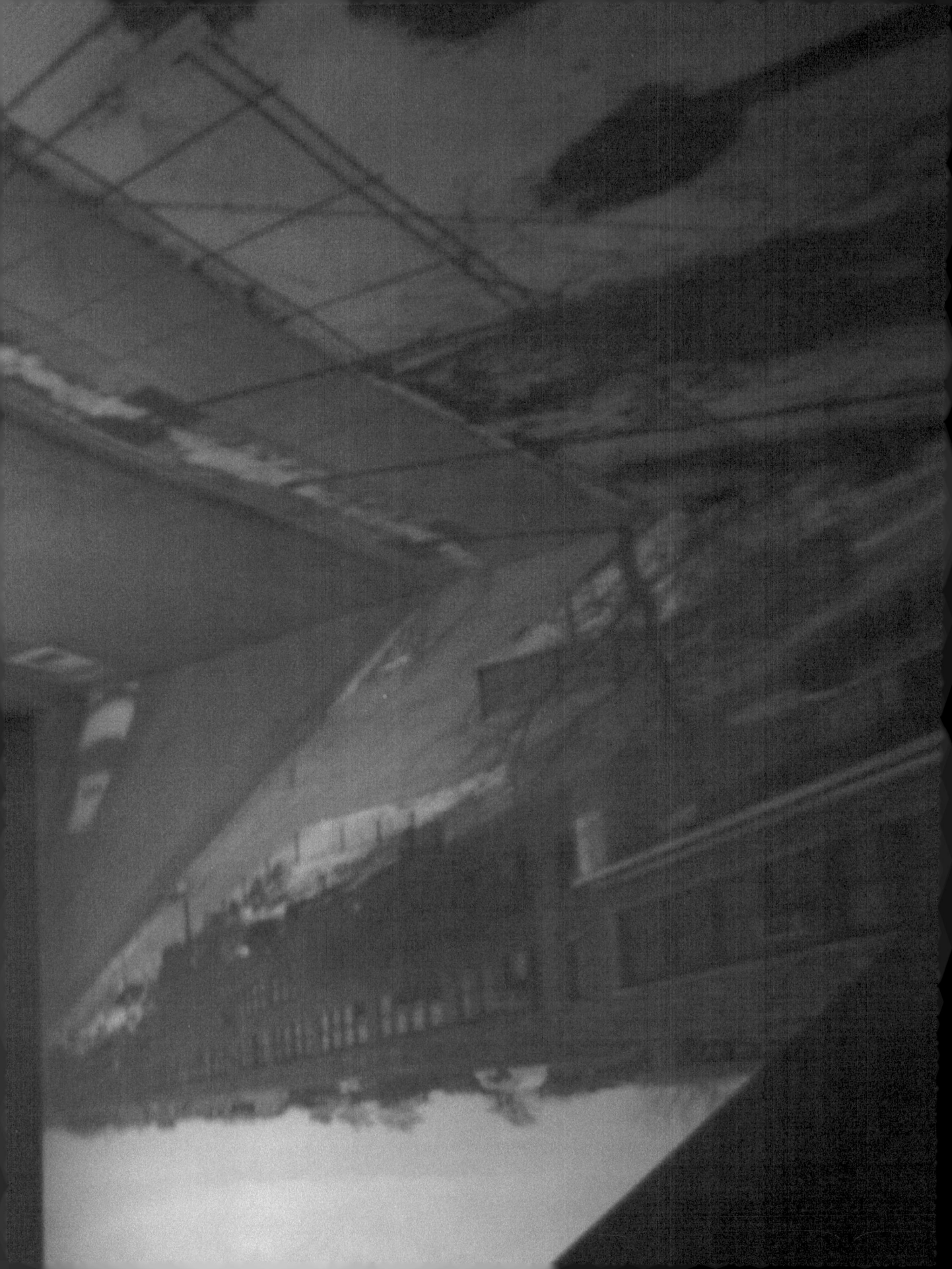

Camera Obscura

As Though We Were Never Here

For the most part, photographs travel through time in a semi-static state. A living photograph, though, can be seen when you enter a camera obscura. A room sized camera chamber works by blocking out all of the external light and opening a small aperture. When this is done a photographic image of the outside world appears on the inside wall.

"As Though We Were Never Here" is a camera obscura installation with two apertures (one facing the south and one facing the west). The result is an overlapping image that changes with time and is weighted from one image to the other depending on the time of day. These images are projected onto two semi-monochromatic (painted) canvases. The result is an examination of the solidity of painting and the transience of the living photograph.

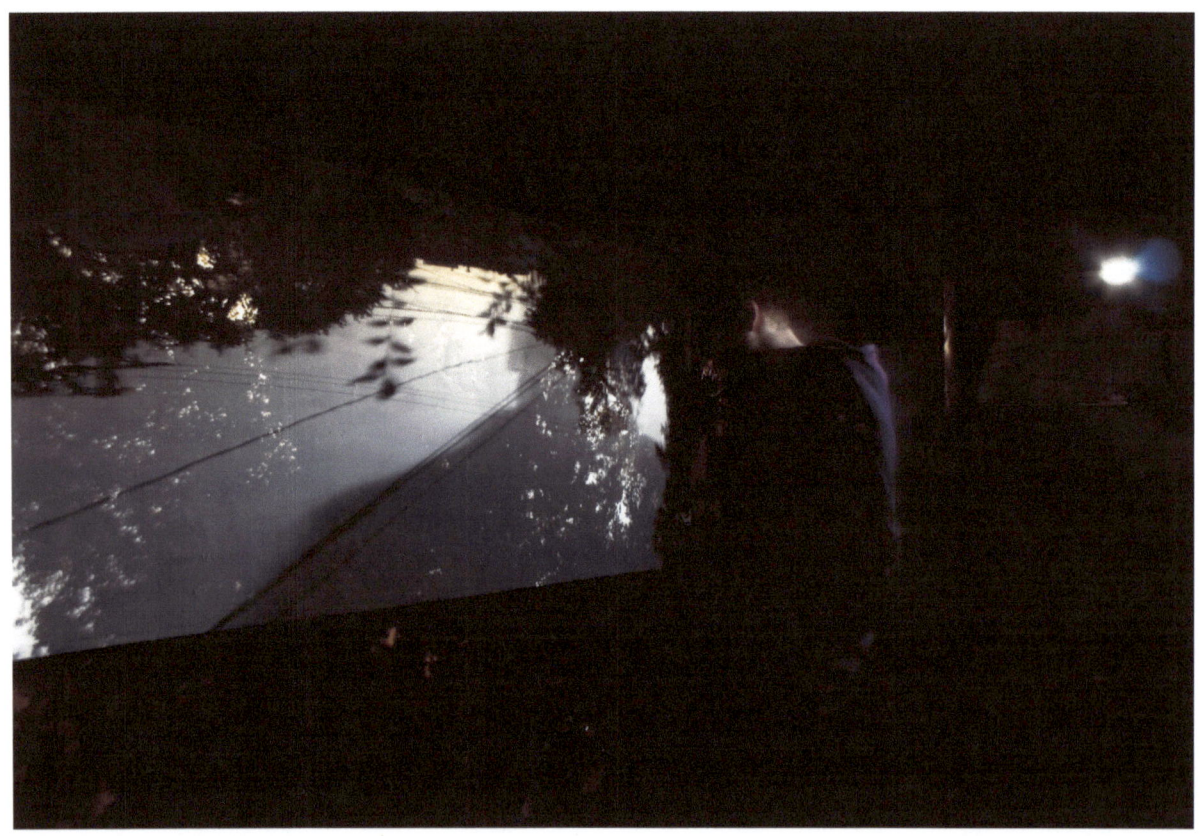

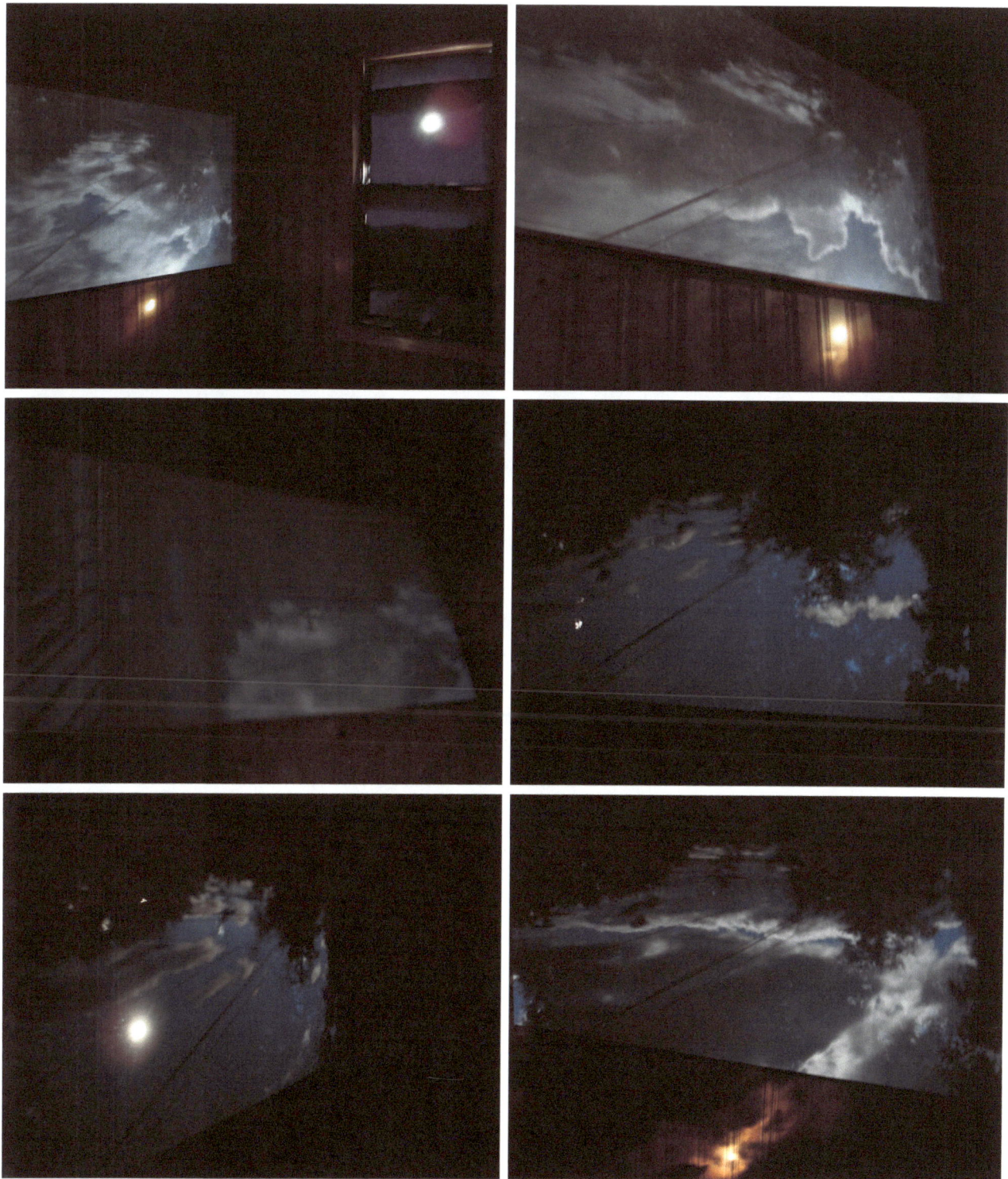

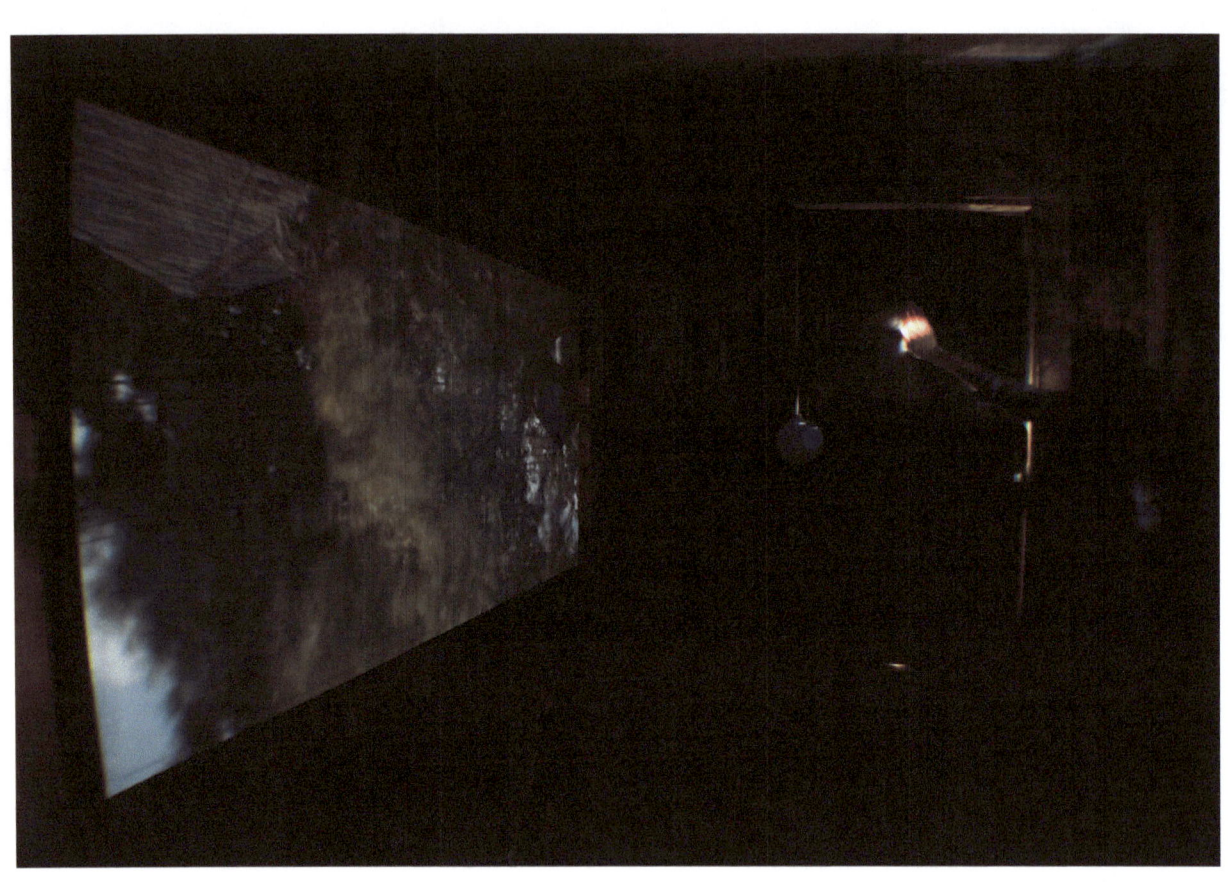

35.

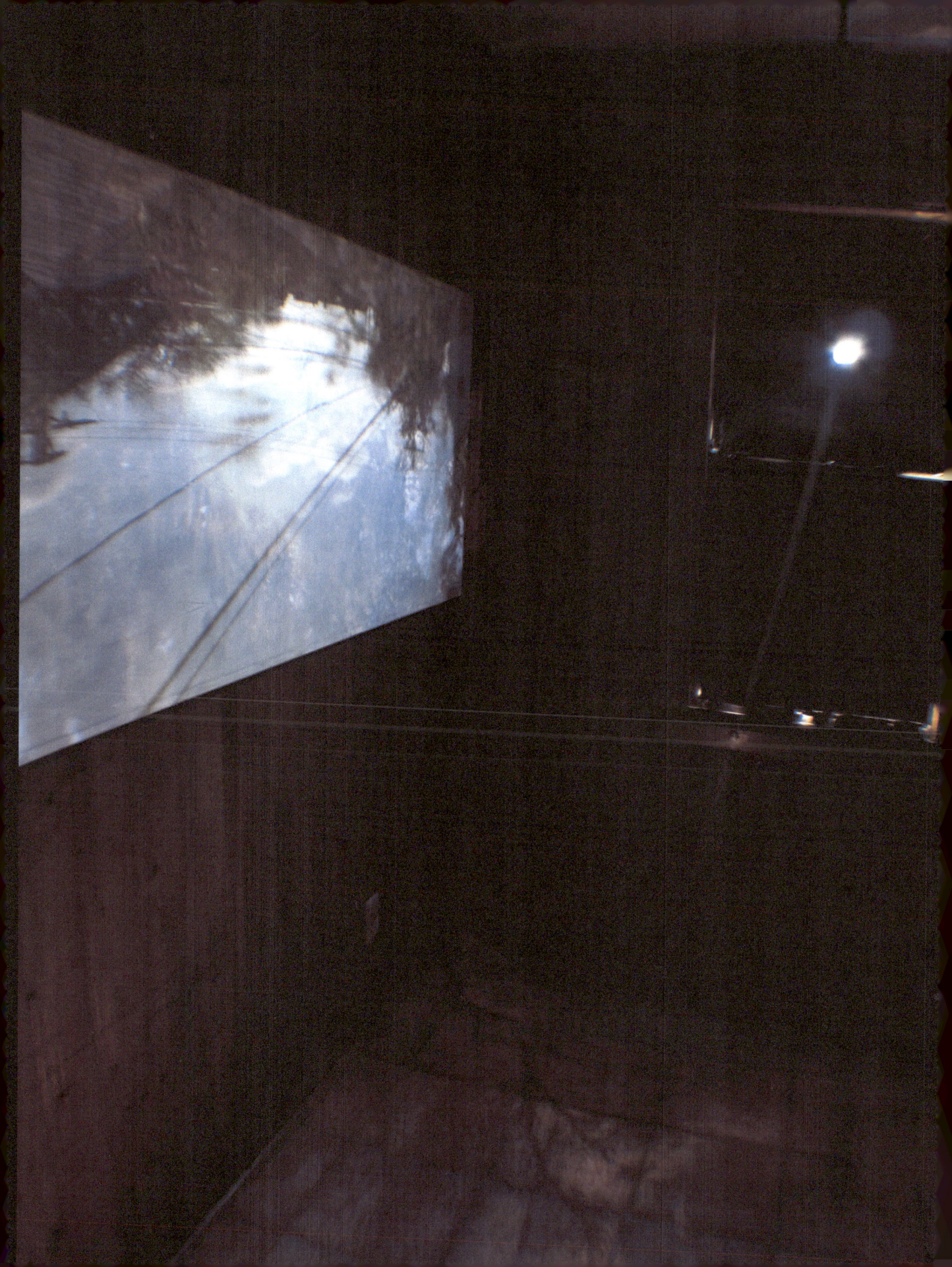

Image List

Painting
1) "Öd' und leer das Meer" Oil and Acrylic on Canvas 64"x 42" 2008.
2) (detail) "Öd' und leer das Meer"
3) "Thánatos" Oil and Acrylic on Canvas 18" x 20" 2009.
4) "Breyfrogle" Oil and Acrylic on Canvas 12" x 36" 2010.
5) "This, Sanctuary" Oil and Acrylic on Canvas 84" x 58" 2010.
6) (detail) "This, Sanctuary"
7) "Perambulate (Carrier)" Oil and Acrylic on Canvas 22" x 22" 2009.
8) "The Tenants" Oil and Acrylic on Canvas 36" x 56" 2009.
9) "The Harvester" Oil and Acrylic on Canvas 12" x 12" 2009.
10) "This Weight Has Fallen" Oil and Acrylic on Canvas 48" x 36" 2010.
11) "Principium Individuationis" Oil and Acrylic on Canvas 16"x18" 2008.
12) "Sisters" Oil and Acrylic on Canvas 8" x 16" 2010.
13) "The Identity of Ghosts" Oil and Acrylic on Canvas 20" x 16" 2008.
14) "Cenotaph and the Sea" Oil and Acrylic on Canvas 20" x 32" 2009.
15) "Give" Oil and Acrylic on Board 20" x 24" 2010.
16) "I See Now..." Oil and Acrylic on Canvas 30" x 24" 2009.
17) "Through" Oil and Acrylic on Canvas 10"x 8" 2009.
18) "Search (Charon)" Oil and Acrylic on Canvas 12"x12" 2009.
19) "The Deep (865)" Oil and Acrylic on Canvas 100" x 38" 2009.

Photo
20) "(Untitled)" Archival Inkjet Print 2010.
21) "(Untitled)" Archival Inkjet Print 2010.
22) "(Untitled)" Archival Inkjet Print 2010.
23) "(Untitled)" Archival Inkjet Print 2010.
24) "The Mason Family" Archival Inkjet Print 2008.
25) "From the Train" Archival Inkjet Print 2009.
26) "Home" Archival Inkjet Print 2009.
27) "Sisters" Archival Inkjet Print 2010.
28) "(Untitled)" Archival Inkjet Print 2010.
29) "(Untitled)" Archival Inkjet Print 2010.
30) "Think of Dying" Archival Inkjet Print 2009.
31) "Resolutions" Archival Inkjet Print 2009.
32) "Three Visions (Landscape as Ghost)" Archival Inkjet Print 2010.

Camera Obscura

33) "As Though We Were Never Here" Installation 2010.

34) "As Though We Were Never Here" Installation 2010. Photos courtesy of Jennifer Hines.

35) "As Though We Were Never Here" Installation 2010.

36) "As Though We Were Never Here" Installation 2010.

Studio

37) Studio 2010.

38) Studio 2010. Photo courtesy of Lillian Weiss.

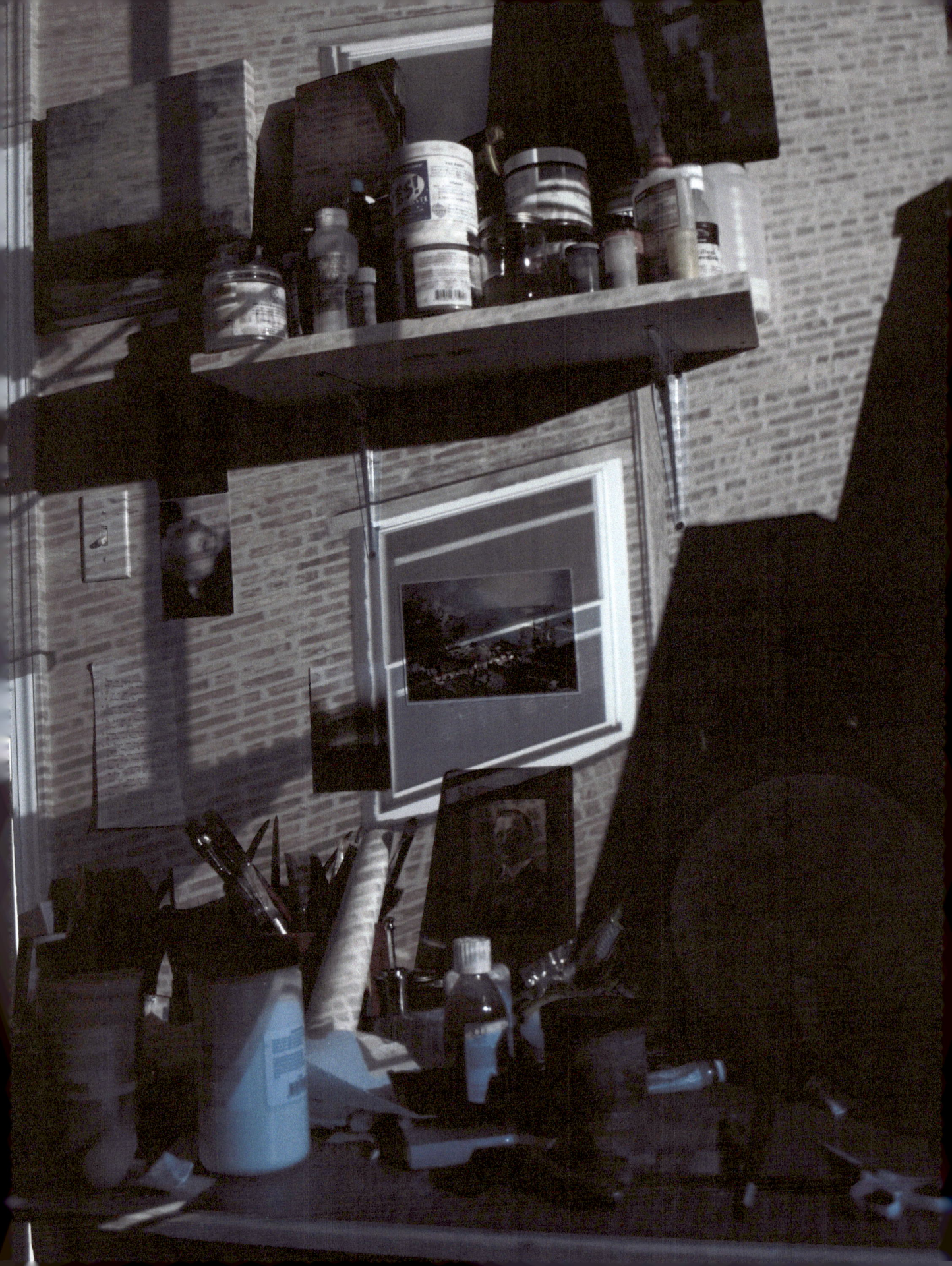

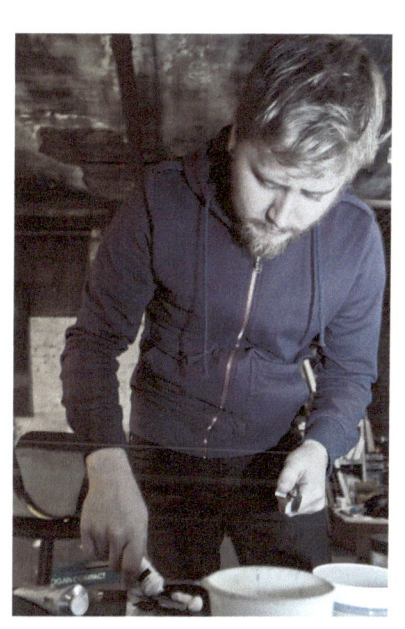

www.ingramcontent.com/pod-product-compliance
Lightning Source LLC
Chambersburg PA
CBHW050812180526
45159CB00004B/1634